Sedona Bucket List 2024-2025: Your

Ultimate Guide to Must-See Attractions, Hidden Gems, and Unforgettable Experiences in Sedona.

BY

Louis S. Harper

TABLE OF CONTENT

MAP OF SEDONA

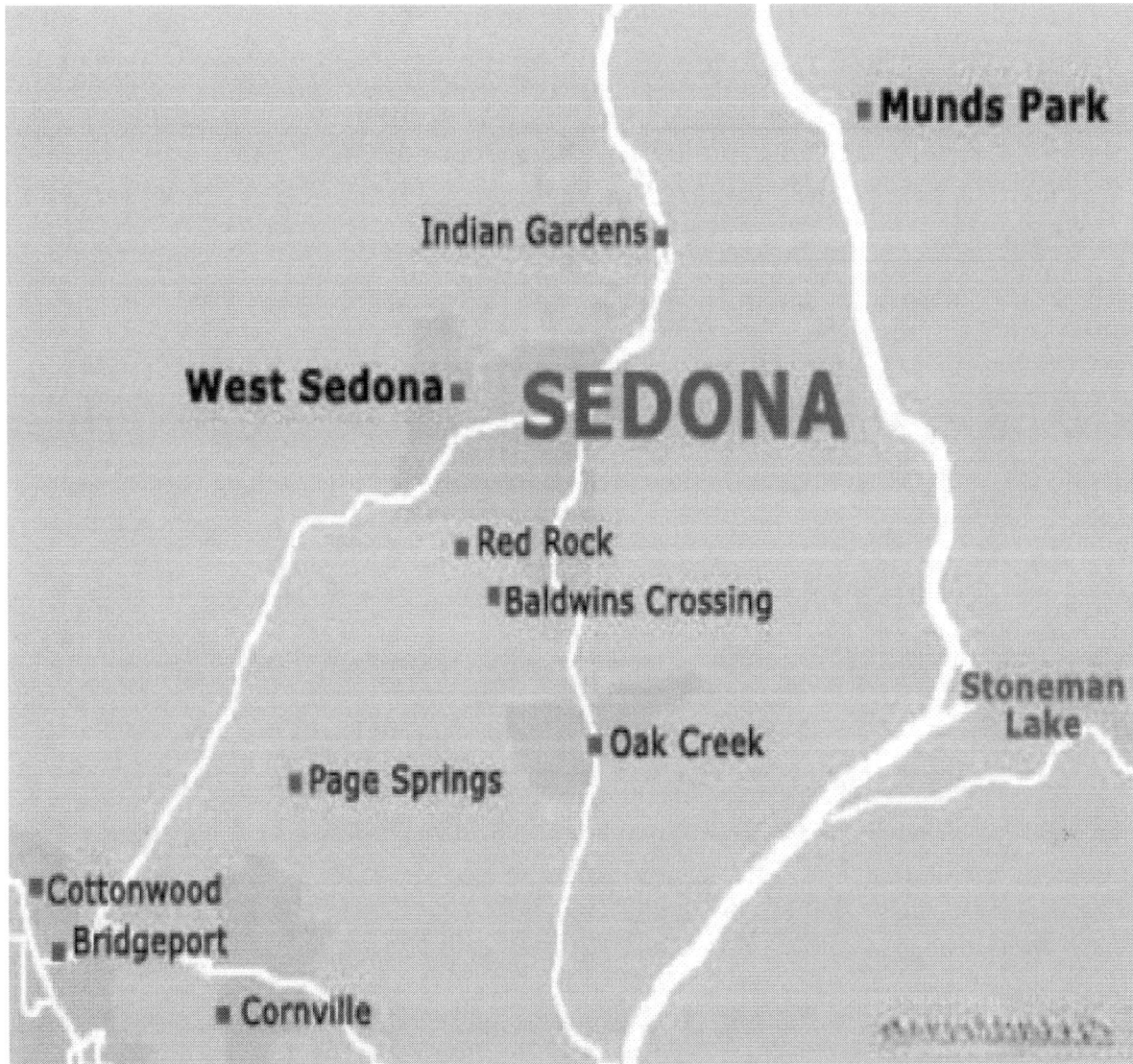

Welcome to Sedona

Nestled amidst Arizona's stunning red rock landscapes, Sedona is a destination like no other. Whether you're seeking outdoor adventures, spiritual renewal, or simply a peaceful escape, Sedona has something for everyone. Known for its vibrant arts community, rich Native American history, and breathtaking natural beauty, this desert town offers an unparalleled experience for every type of traveler. Prepare to be enchanted by its scenic trails, awe-inspiring vortex sites, and world-class dining and shopping. In this guide, you'll discover the best Sedona has to offer, from hidden gems to must-see attractions.

Introduction to Sedona

Sedona isn't just another picturesque destination—it's a place where nature and culture seamlessly intertwine. Located in northern Arizona, Sedona is renowned for its striking red rock formations, which transform into mesmerizing shades of crimson and orange during sunrise and sunset. The town itself is a hub for artists, spiritual seekers, and nature lovers, all drawn to its otherworldly landscape and peaceful energy. Whether you're exploring ancient Native American ruins, browsing the many art galleries, or hiking through one of the many canyons, Sedona promises an unforgettable journey.

With its mild climate, Sedona is a year-round destination, making it perfect for both summer getaways and winter retreats. You can enjoy outdoor activities like hiking, mountain biking, and stargazing under some of the clearest skies in the country. More than just its natural allure, Sedona is also home to luxurious spas, holistic healing centers, and a burgeoning culinary scene that offers everything from Southwest-inspired dishes to organic, farm-to-table meals.

Why Sedona Should Be on Your Bucket List

There are countless reasons why Sedona deserves a place on your bucket list. First and foremost, the landscape alone is worth the trip. The towering red rock formations that surround the town create a dramatic backdrop that changes throughout the day, offering perfect photo opportunities at every turn. Popular spots like Cathedral Rock, Bell Rock, and Devil's Bridge attract hikers and photographers from around the world.

For those with a spiritual inclination, Sedona is also famous for its energy vortexes—spiritual hotspots believed to offer healing and enlightenment. Visitors often come seeking meditation, energy healing, and personal transformation. But even if you're not seeking spiritual experiences, the peaceful environment of Sedona can offer a sense of renewal and relaxation that few other places can.

Sedona is also a haven for art enthusiasts. The town boasts over 80 galleries and shops, showcasing the work of local artisans, from Native American crafts to contemporary pieces. The renowned Tlaquepaque Arts & Crafts Village is a must-visit for anyone looking to immerse themselves in Sedona's vibrant arts scene.

In addition, Sedona's proximity to other attractions like the Grand Canyon, Oak Creek Canyon, and the Verde Valley makes it an ideal base for exploring more of Arizona's natural wonders. Whether you're planning a weekend getaway or a longer stay, Sedona offers an experience that combines adventure, relaxation, and cultural enrichment in one breathtaking package. Don't miss your chance to explore this magical desert oasis.

Best Times to Visit Sedona

Sedona is a captivating destination that shines throughout the year, but the timing of your visit can shape your experience depending on what you wish to explore. With its majestic red rock scenery, comfortable weather, and a calendar full of cultural events, Sedona is an ideal getaway in any season. By understanding the seasonal weather and notable events, you can plan a trip that perfectly aligns with your interests, whether it's outdoor activities, artistic events, or vibrant festivals.

Sedona's Weather and Seasons

Sedona's climate is generally mild, but each season offers distinct opportunities for exploration. Here's what you can expect during different times of the year:

Spring (March to May):
Spring is arguably the most popular time to visit Sedona, with blooming wildflowers and moderate temperatures between 60°F and 80°F (15°C to 27°C). This season is ideal for outdoor adventures like hiking and biking, as the red rocks come alive with color and the weather is perfect for exploring. However, due to the popularity of this time, it's wise to plan ahead, as accommodations fill up quickly.

Summer (June to August):
Summer brings warmer weather, with daytime highs reaching 90°F to 100°F (32°C to 38°C), but early mornings and evenings remain comfortable. If you're an early riser, this is a great time to explore Sedona's outdoor attractions before the heat sets in. Monsoon season, typically in late July and August, adds a refreshing twist to the landscape with afternoon showers and temporary waterfalls, making the red rock scenery even more dramatic.

Fall (September to November):
Fall competes with spring as the best time to visit. Temperatures hover around 60°F to 80°F (15°C to 27°C), and the autumn hues of Oak Creek Canyon add a vibrant touch to the scenery. With fewer crowds than spring, fall provides a more peaceful experience, perfect for hiking or enjoying Sedona's renowned wineries during the grape harvest season.

Winter (December to February):
Though winter temperatures can be chilly at night, daytime averages around 50°F to 60°F (10°C to 15°C), making it a great time for those seeking a quieter, more serene visit. On rare occasions, snow may dust the red rocks, offering stunning, postcard-like views. For budget-conscious travelers, winter is a great time to take advantage of lower hotel rates while enjoying Sedona's peaceful beauty.

Top Events and Festivals

Sedona is not only known for its natural beauty but also for its vibrant arts and cultural scene. Throughout the year, Sedona hosts a variety of exciting events and festivals that showcase its unique community and traditions. Here are some of the top annual events:

Sedona International Film Festival (February):
This prestigious film festival draws filmmakers and film lovers from across the globe for a week of screenings, workshops, and discussions. Featuring over 150 films in different genres, it's the perfect event for anyone passionate about cinema.

Sedona Mountain Bike Festival (March):
Outdoor enthusiasts flock to this three-day festival, which includes bike demos, live music, food, and access to Sedona's stunning mountain biking trails. It's a must-visit for anyone looking to experience the breathtaking terrain on two wheels.

Sedona Yoga Festival (April):
Held in one of the world's most spiritual locations, the Sedona Yoga Festival offers a blend of yoga sessions, meditation, and wellness workshops, making it an ideal event for those seeking personal growth and tranquility in the stunning surroundings of Sedona's red rocks.

Sedona Winefest (September):
This lively event celebrates Arizona's growing wine industry, featuring wine tastings from local vineyards, live music, and an art marketplace. It's a fantastic way to enjoy Sedona's beautiful fall weather while sampling some of the region's best wines.

Day of the Dead Celebration (October-November):
Held at Tlaquepaque Arts & Crafts Village, Sedona's Day of the Dead event is a vibrant and heartfelt celebration honoring deceased loved ones. With altars, live

music, and traditional food, visitors are invited to participate in this rich cultural experience.

Red Rocks Music Festival (November):
This classical music festival draws world-renowned musicians to Sedona for a series of intimate concerts in stunning settings. It's a must for music lovers who appreciate live performances in a breathtaking backdrop.

RunSedona Marathon (February):
For athletes, the RunSedona Marathon offers the chance to race through one of the most scenic landscapes in the world. The event caters to all skill levels, with 5K, 10K, and full marathon options, all set against the stunning red rock formations.

Sedona Arts Festival (October):
This two-day event highlights the work of over 100 artists, featuring paintings, sculptures, jewelry, and photography. It's a great way to explore Sedona's artistic community while finding unique pieces of art inspired by the region's natural beauty.

Whether you're visiting Sedona for its outdoor adventures, spiritual renewal, or to enjoy its rich artistic culture, aligning your visit with the best season or festival can elevate your experience. Each time of year and event offers something special, ensuring that Sedona will leave you with unforgettable memories.

Getting to Sedona

Sedona, Arizona, is a globally recognized destination known for its breathtaking red rock formations, vibrant arts culture, and spiritual significance. Although located in a somewhat remote area, reaching Sedona is relatively simple, with multiple travel options available to suit different preferences. Whether you choose to fly, drive, or use public transportation, Sedona is accessible for all types of travelers. Once you arrive, there are several ways to get around, including renting a car, biking, or taking part in guided walking tours. This section provides a detailed guide on how to reach Sedona and how to navigate once you've arrived.

Travel Options: Flights, Driving, and Public Transport

Flights to Sedona

Although Sedona doesn't have its own major airport, it can be easily accessed via several nearby airports. The most convenient option is flying into **Phoenix Sky Harbor International Airport (PHX)**, approximately 120 miles (193 kilometers) from Sedona. As Arizona's largest airport, it serves a wide range of domestic and international flights, making it an ideal hub for travelers worldwide. From Phoenix, you can rent a car, take a shuttle, or arrange private transport to Sedona.

Another option is **Flagstaff Pulliam Airport (FLG)**, which is only 40 miles (64 kilometers) from Sedona. Though smaller with fewer flight options, it offers a quicker drive to Sedona and serves regional flights, making it a more convenient entry point for some travelers.

Alternatively, **Las Vegas McCarran International Airport (LAS)**, located about 275 miles (442 kilometers) away, can serve as a longer but scenic starting point. Many travelers use this airport for an extended road trip, enjoying the desert landscapes en route to Sedona.

Driving to Sedona

Driving to Sedona is an excellent choice, particularly for those who enjoy road trips. Situated off Arizona's Highway 89A, the journey offers some of the most beautiful scenic views. From **Phoenix**, the drive to Sedona takes about two hours along

Interstate 17 North and Highway 179, which brings you directly into Sedona with stunning views along the way.

From **Flagstaff**, the drive is even shorter, taking just under an hour via Highway 89A, a winding road that passes through Oak Creek Canyon. This route offers some of the most picturesque views, with dramatic cliffs and forests surrounding the canyon.

If you're traveling from **Las Vegas or California**, the drive offers a longer but equally rewarding journey. The trip from Las Vegas, following US-93 South and Interstate 40 East toward Flagstaff before connecting to Highway 89A, takes around four and a half hours. Along the way, you'll experience vast desert landscapes that transition into Sedona's iconic red rocks.

Public Transportation to Sedona

For those who prefer not to drive, public transportation to Sedona is also available. Shuttle services such as **Groome Transportation Shuttle** provide regular transfers between **Phoenix Sky Harbor International Airport** and Sedona, offering a convenient, stress-free way to reach the town. The shuttle ride usually takes about two and a half hours, depending on traffic.

From **Flagstaff**, you can use the Mountain Line bus service to travel to Sedona, though it may not be as direct or frequent. Additionally, if you prefer train travel, **Amtrak Southwest Chief** makes a stop in Flagstaff, from where you can either rent a car or take local transportation to Sedona.

Navigating Sedona: Car Rentals, Biking, and Walking Tours

Once you've arrived in Sedona, exploring the area is easy with various transportation options available.

Car Rentals

Renting a car is the most convenient and flexible way to navigate Sedona, especially if you plan to visit nearby attractions like Oak Creek Canyon or Red Rock State Park. Numerous car rental companies operate out of **Phoenix Sky Harbor**, **Flagstaff**, and within Sedona itself. Having a car allows you to explore Sedona's key landmarks, such as Bell Rock, Cathedral Rock, and the Chapel of the Holy Cross, at your own pace.

Many of Sedona's top attractions are spread out, making a car essential for those wanting to explore the entire area. Parking is available at most trailheads and landmarks, though it can get crowded during peak times. Make sure to get a **Red Rock Pass** if you're parking in designated areas within **Coconino National Forest**, as it's required for some trailheads and viewpoints.

Biking in Sedona

For a more eco-friendly and active way to explore, biking is an excellent option. Sedona is known for its outstanding mountain biking trails, but there are also more relaxed paths for casual riders. Local shops offer bike rentals, and guided tours are available for those who want to explore the red rock terrain with the help of an expert guide.

The **Bell Rock Pathway** is a popular route for biking, offering beautiful views of Sedona's red rock formations and accessible to riders of all levels. For more experienced cyclists, the **Sedona Mountain Bike Park** offers challenging terrain. Electric bike rentals are also available, providing an easier way to explore more of the area with less effort.

Walking Tours

Sedona is a perfect town for walking, offering a variety of walking tours that allow you to fully take in its beauty. Several guided walking tours are available, focusing on Sedona's history, arts, and culture. Highlights include tours of the **Tlaquepaque Arts & Crafts Village**, the **Sedona Heritage Museum**, and various local galleries.

For those drawn to Sedona's spiritual side, guided **vortex tours** take visitors to energy hotspots believed to offer healing and spiritual renewal. These tours provide opportunities for meditation and reflection in the serene beauty of Sedona's natural surroundings.

The town of Sedona itself, particularly areas like **Uptown Sedona**, is walkable and offers many attractions, including shops, galleries, and cafes. While some attractions require transportation due to distance, much of Sedona's charm can be explored on foot once you're in the main areas.

Top Must-See Attractions in Sedona

Sedona is home to some of the most striking natural landmarks and cultural sights, making it a top destination for visitors seeking adventure, tranquility, or spiritual experiences. This section highlights four of Sedona's most popular attractions: Cathedral Rock, Bell Rock, Chapel of the Holy Cross, and Red Rock Crossing. Whether you're looking for breathtaking hikes, spiritual reflection, or simply stunning views, these spots will make your visit to Sedona truly unforgettable.

1. Cathedral Rock

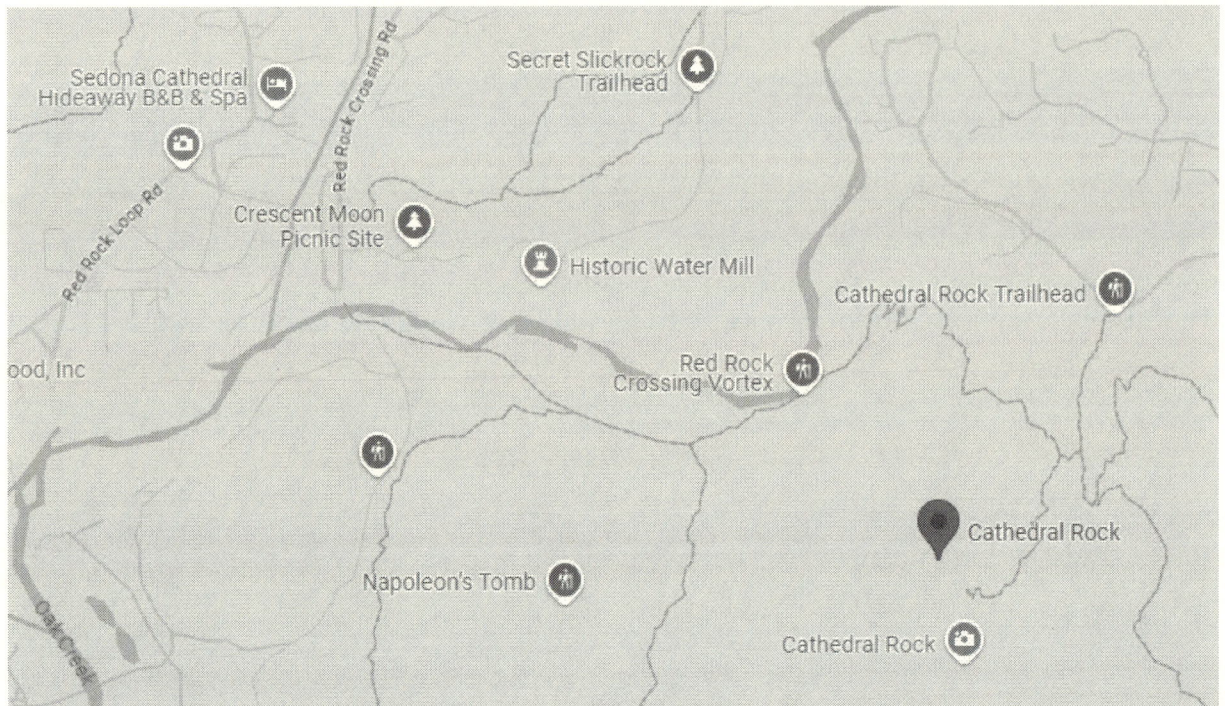

Highlights:

Cathedral Rock is one of the most iconic formations in Sedona, known for its towering red spires and breathtaking views. Located in the Coconino National Forest, it's a must-see for hikers and spiritual seekers alike. The hike to the summit is short but challenging, with a steep ascent and an elevation gain of 740 feet. The round-trip hike is about 1.2 miles, and the panoramic views from the top are well worth the effort, offering incredible vistas of the surrounding red rocks and valleys.

Cathedral Rock is also a spiritual vortex, making it a popular destination for meditation and those seeking inner peace. The scenic backdrop and peaceful atmosphere make this an ideal spot for nature lovers and photographers, especially during sunrise and sunset when the rocks glow in vibrant hues.

Pricing:

To access Cathedral Rock, a **Red Rock Pass** is required, with the following options:

- $5 for a day pass
- $15 for a weekly pass
- $20 for an annual pass
  These passes can be purchased at vending machines at the trailhead or online.

Location:
Back O' Beyond Road, Sedona, AZ 86336
Trailhead Map

2. Bell Rock

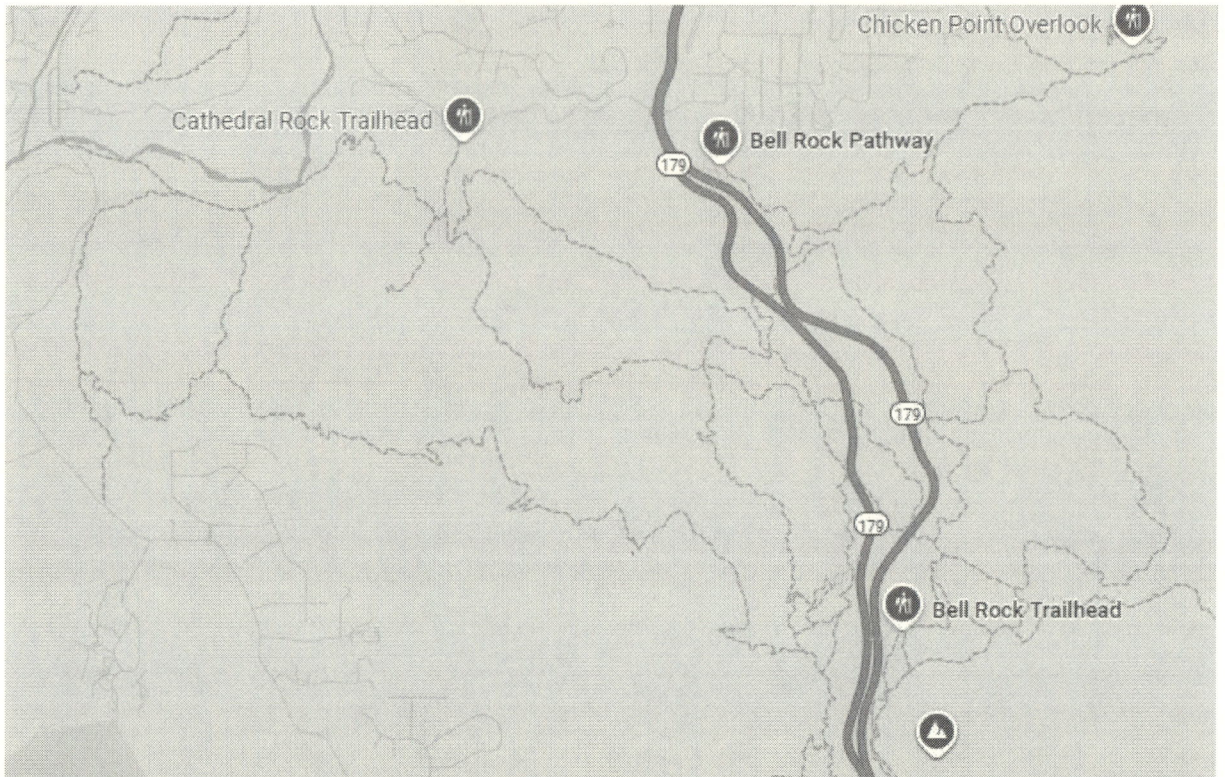

Highlights:

Bell Rock, with its distinctive bell shape, is another iconic Sedona landmark located along Highway 179. It offers a variety of hiking trails that range from easy walks around the base to more challenging climbs up the rock itself. As one of Sedona's famed vortex sites, Bell Rock attracts those seeking spiritual experiences, as well as outdoor enthusiasts. It's a popular spot for hiking, mountain biking, and photography, especially at sunrise or sunset when the light enhances the red hues of the rocks.

The **Bell Rock Pathway** is an easy 3.6-mile trail perfect for families or casual hikers, offering spectacular views of Bell Rock and Courthouse Butte. More adventurous hikers can explore the steeper, more rugged areas as they ascend the rock.

Pricing:

A **Red Rock Pass** is required for parking at Bell Rock:

- $5 for a day pass
- $15 for a weekly pass
- $20 for an annual pass

Location:
Bell Rock Trailhead, Sedona, AZ 86336
Map & Directions

3. Chapel of the Holy Cross

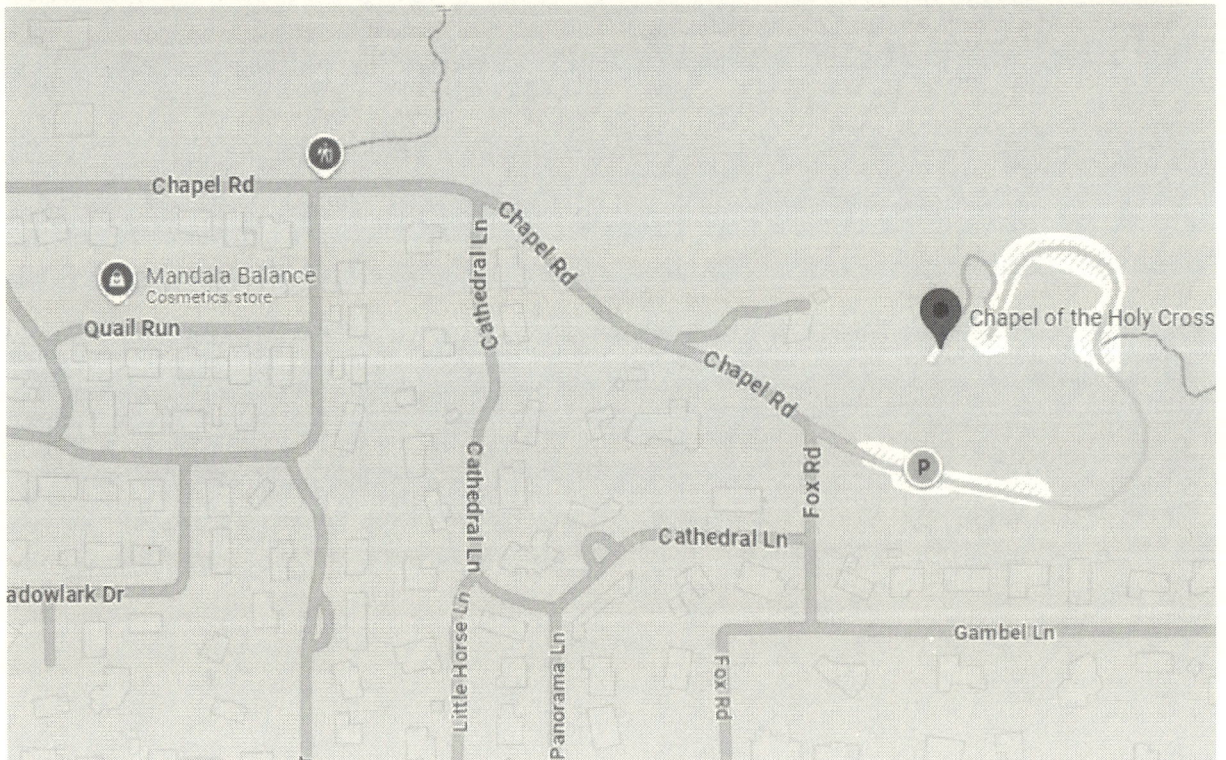

Highlights:
Perched dramatically on a red rock formation, the **Chapel of the Holy Cross** is an architectural marvel that blends seamlessly into the surrounding landscape. Designed by Marguerite Brunswig Staude and completed in 1956, the chapel's modernist design and towering cross make it a striking feature in Sedona. The chapel is not only a place of worship but also a peaceful spot for contemplation and reflection, offering stunning panoramic views of the red rock formations below.

Visitors can admire the unique architecture and enjoy the tranquil setting, both inside the chapel and on its surrounding grounds. The location provides one of the best vantage points for sweeping views of Sedona's natural beauty, making it a favorite for photographers and visitors seeking a moment of serenity.

Pricing:
Free entry (donations appreciated)

Location:
780 Chapel Rd, Sedona, AZ 86336
Map & Directions

Website:
https://chapeloftheholycross.com

4. Red Rock Crossing (Crescent Moon Ranch)

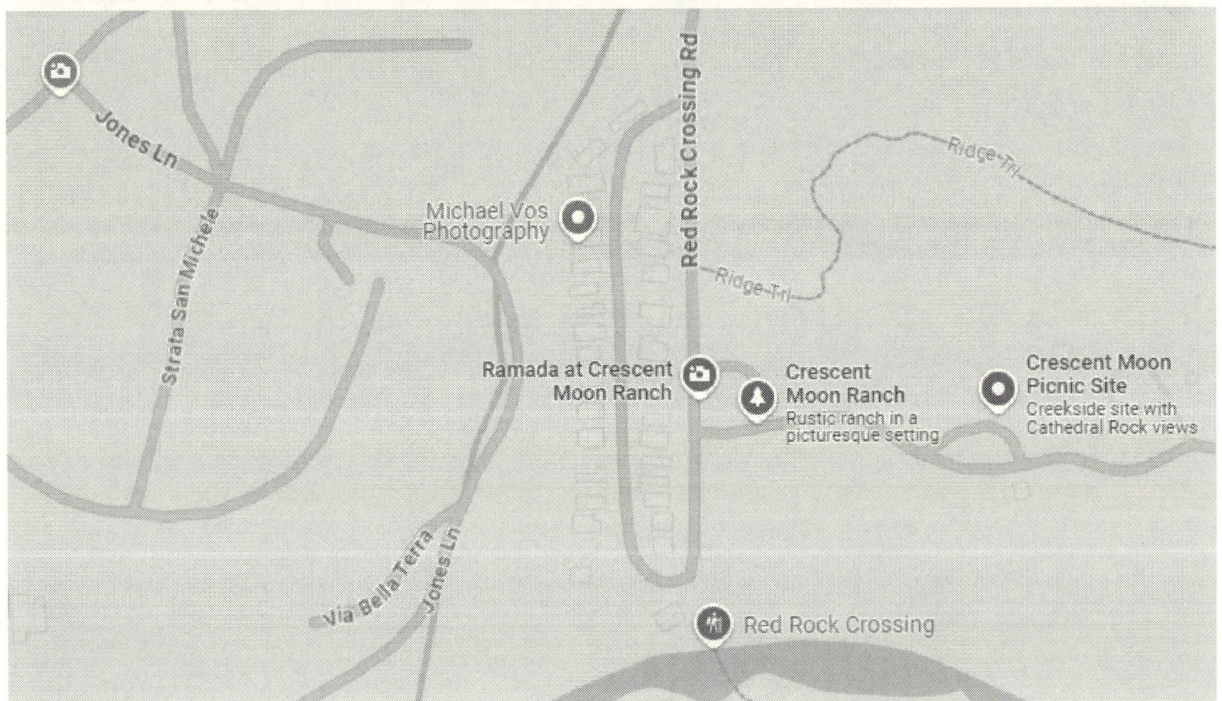

Highlights:

Red Rock Crossing, situated within **Crescent Moon Ranch**, is one of Sedona's most photographed spots, thanks to its iconic view of Cathedral Rock reflected in Oak Creek. This peaceful location is perfect for easy walks, picnics, and leisurely days by the creek. Families, photographers, and hikers alike flock to this area for its natural beauty and tranquil ambiance.

The **Crescent Moon Picnic Area** offers a scenic spot for meals, with tables overlooking the creek. Short trails lead visitors to swimming holes, relaxing spots by the water, and **Buddha Beach**, a popular meditation spot. Red Rock Crossing is especially magical in the late afternoon, when the light turns the red rocks golden.

Pricing:
Entry to Crescent Moon Ranch costs:

- $11 per vehicle (for up to 5 people)
- $2 per walk-in or additional passenger

Location:
Crescent Moon Ranch, 333 Red Rock Crossing Rd, Sedona, AZ 86336
Map & Directions

Sedona's top attractions offer a diverse mix of stunning natural landscapes, spiritual experiences, and architectural wonders. Whether you're scaling Cathedral Rock, discovering the serenity of Bell Rock, or visiting the awe-inspiring Chapel of the Holy Cross, these must-see destinations are sure to enhance your journey through this enchanting desert town. Don't forget to bring your camera—Sedona's beauty is truly unforgettable.

Hiking and Outdoor Adventures in Sedona

Sedona's breathtaking red rock landscapes make it a haven for outdoor lovers, offering countless opportunities for hiking, off-road adventures, and enjoying panoramic viewpoints. Whether you're a seasoned hiker or prefer guided excursions, Sedona promises memorable experiences in nature. This section highlights the top hiking trails, scenic viewpoints, and popular jeep tours for those seeking adventure in Sedona.

Best Hiking Trails in Sedona

Sedona boasts an impressive range of hiking trails, suitable for various skill levels. From easy walks to challenging hikes, these trails showcase the area's iconic red rock formations, canyons, and unique desert scenery. Below are some of Sedona's best hiking trails:

1. Devil's Bridge Trail

Highlights:
One of Sedona's most renowned hikes, **Devil's Bridge**, leads to a natural sandstone arch offering spectacular views. This moderate 4.2-mile round-trip trail is mostly flat until the final ascent, where steep steps lead to the bridge. The stunning views

at the top and the chance to walk across the arch make this hike a must for any visitor.

Pricing:
A **Red Rock Pass** is required:

- $5 for a day pass
- $15 for a weekly pass
- $20 for an annual pass

Location:
Devil's Bridge Trailhead, Dry Creek Road, Sedona, AZ 86336
Map & Directions

2. Cathedral Rock Trail

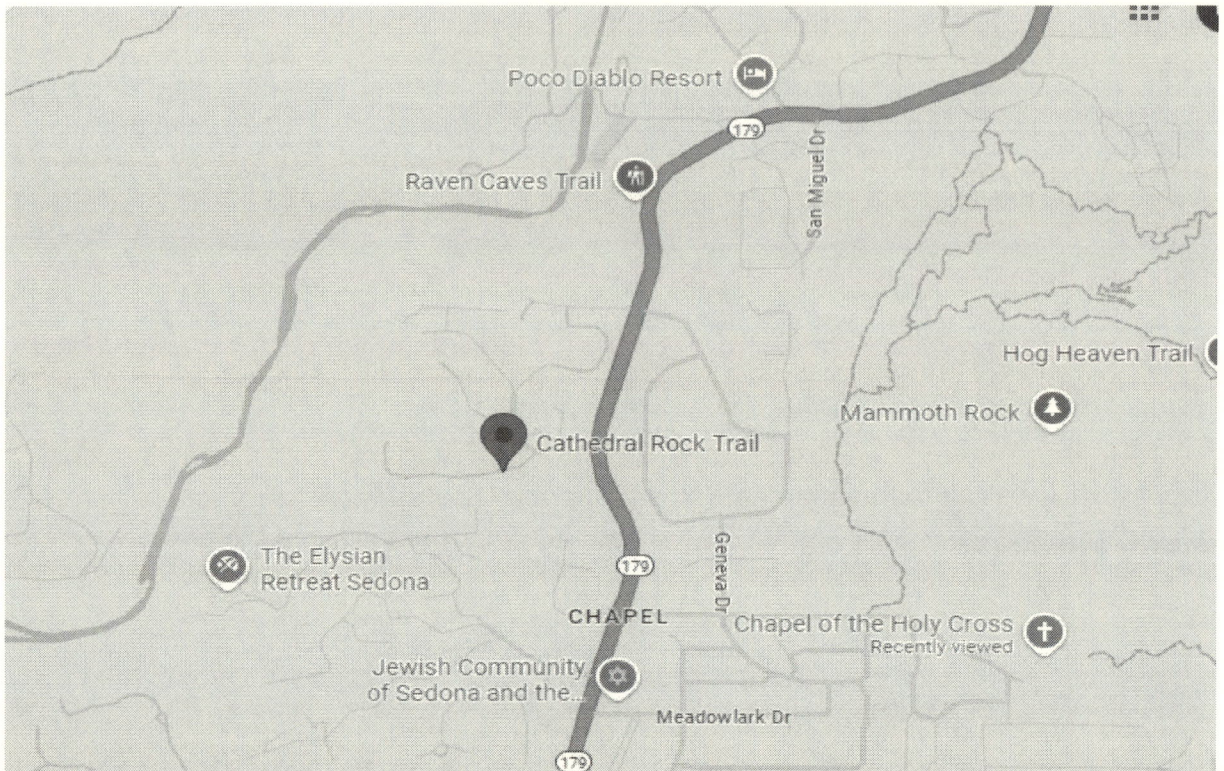

Highlights:

Cathedral Rock Trail is a shorter but steeper hike, offering some of the best panoramic views in Sedona. The trail involves some rock scrambling, and though it's only 1.2 miles round-trip, the steep climb makes it more strenuous. From the top, hikers are rewarded with breathtaking views of the surrounding formations, such as Courthouse Butte and Bell Rock.

Pricing:

A **Red Rock Pass** is required:

- $5 for a day pass
- $15 for a weekly pass
- $20 for an annual pass

Location:

Back O' Beyond Road, Sedona, AZ 86336

Trailhead Map

3. Bell Rock Pathway

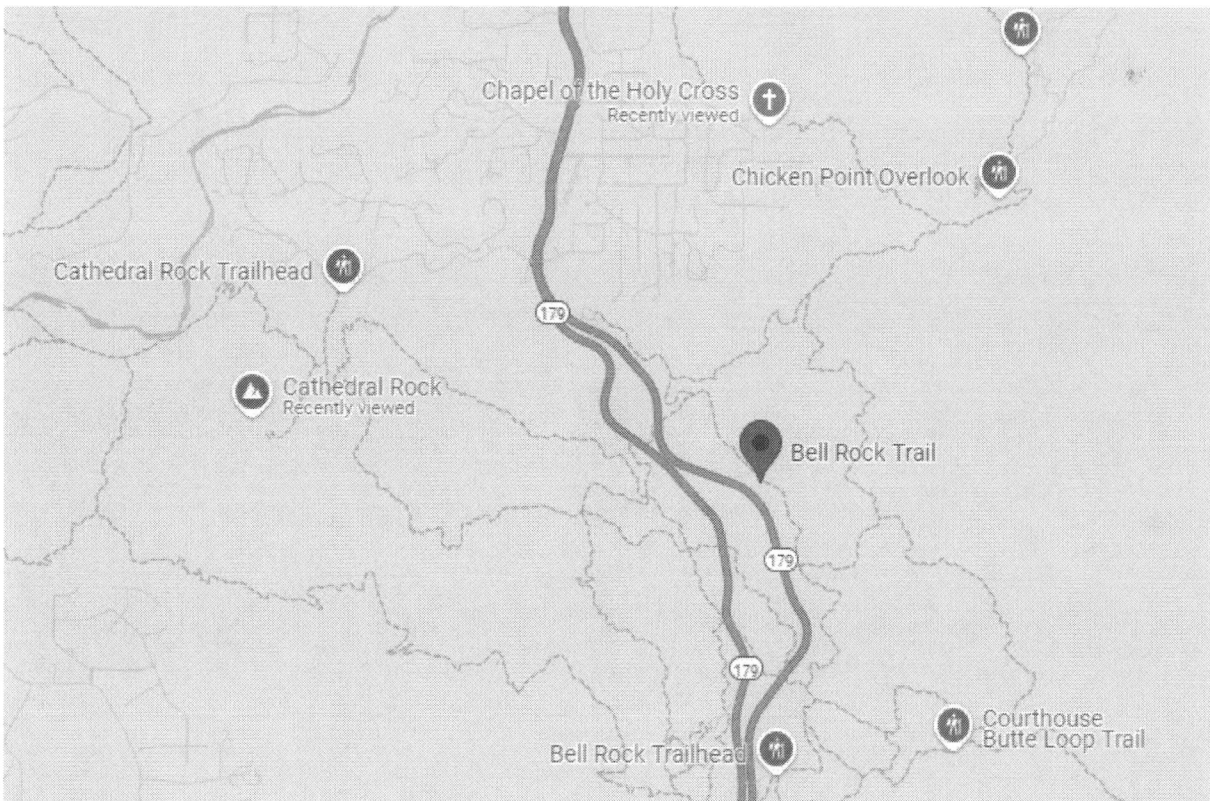

Highlights:
Ideal for beginners or those seeking an easier hike, **Bell Rock Pathway** is a 3.6-mile trail offering relatively flat terrain. It circles **Bell Rock** and provides beautiful views of both Bell Rock and Courthouse Butte. The trail is accessible to hikers of all levels, making it a great option for families and casual explorers. The scenery of Sedona's red rock formations makes it one of the top easy hikes in the area.

Pricing:
A **Red Rock Pass** is required:

- $5 for a day pass
- $15 for a weekly pass
- $20 for an annual pass

Location:
Bell Rock Trailhead, Sedona, AZ 86336
Map & Directions

4. West Fork Trail (Oak Creek Canyon)

Highlights:

For a different experience, **West Fork Trail** in Oak Creek Canyon offers a beautiful hike through a forested canyon with towering cliffs and multiple creek crossings. This 6.5-mile round-trip trail is moderate and offers a cooler, more shaded environment, especially in fall when the colors change. It's one of Sedona's most popular hikes, offering a lush, green contrast to the red rocks.

Pricing:

Parking costs:

- $11 per vehicle
- $2 per additional passenger or walk-in

Location:

West Fork Trailhead, Oak Creek Canyon, Sedona, AZ 86336
Map & Directions

Scenic Vistas and Lookout Points

Sedona offers numerous scenic viewpoints that provide breathtaking panoramas of the surrounding red rock formations and canyons. Below are some top lookout points to take in Sedona's natural beauty:

1. Airport Mesa Overlook

Highlights:
The **Airport Mesa Overlook** is one of the most popular viewpoints in Sedona, offering 360-degree views of the surrounding red rock formations. Located just off Airport Road, this spot is ideal for watching the sunset, where formations like Cathedral Rock, Bell Rock, and Courthouse Butte glow in the evening light.

Pricing:
Parking fee: $3 per vehicle.

Location:
Sedona Airport Scenic Lookout, Airport Road, Sedona, AZ 86336
Map & Directions

2. Schnebly Hill Vista

Highlights:
Schnebly Hill Vista offers stunning views of Sedona's red rock landscape and is accessible via an off-road drive along Schnebly Hill Road. This more secluded viewpoint provides jaw-dropping vistas of the surrounding scenery and is a great place for both daytime views and stargazing.

Pricing:
Free access, though a high-clearance vehicle is recommended.

Location:
Schnebly Hill Road, Sedona, AZ 86336
Map & Directions

3. Chapel of the Holy Cross Viewpoint

Highlights:

Besides being an architectural marvel, the **Chapel of the Holy Cross** also offers a fantastic vantage point for panoramic views of Sedona. The elevated location provides unobstructed views of the surrounding red rock formations, including Cathedral Rock, making it a perfect spot for contemplation and photography.

Pricing:

Free entry (donations appreciated).

Location:

780 Chapel Rd, Sedona, AZ 86336

Map & Directions

Website:

https://chapeloftheholycross.com

Jeep Tours and Off-Roading Adventures

For visitors looking for an adrenaline rush, Sedona is famous for its Jeep tours and off-road excursions. These guided tours allow you to explore the rugged wilderness areas, offering access to remote spots that regular vehicles can't reach.

1. Pink Jeep Tours

Highlights:

Pink Jeep Tours is a renowned tour company offering a range of off-roading adventures through Sedona's red rock terrain. Their most popular tour, **Broken Arrow**, takes you through dramatic rock formations and deep into the backcountry. The experienced guides provide insights into Sedona's history, geology, and wildlife, making it a thrilling and educational experience.

Pricing:

Tours range from $125 to $175 per person, depending on the tour length and type.

Location:

204 N State Route 89A, Sedona, AZ 86336

Map & Directions

2. Red Rock Western Jeep Tours

Highlights:

Red Rock Western Jeep Tours offers a variety of scenic and historical off-road tours. Their **Coyote Canyons** tour is perfect for exploring Sedona's hidden trails and scenic landscapes, while the **Ancient Ruins** tour allows you to explore ancient cliff dwellings, adding a historical element to your adventure.

Pricing:
Tours range from $90 to $150 per person, depending on the tour.

Location:
301 Arizona 89A, Sedona, AZ 86336
Map & Directions

Website:
https://redrockjeep.com

Whether you prefer hiking Sedona's scenic trails, enjoying its stunning viewpoints, or embarking on thrilling Jeep tours, Sedona's outdoor adventures offer something for everyone. With breathtaking views and endless exploration opportunities, it's the perfect destination for nature lovers and adventure seekers alike.

Sedona's Spiritual and Healing Spots

Sedona is renowned for its spiritual energy and healing atmosphere, attracting visitors from around the world seeking inner peace, personal growth, and a deeper connection to nature. Famous for its energy vortexes, wellness retreats, and healing centers, Sedona provides an ideal setting for meditation, relaxation, and spiritual exploration. Whether you're drawn to the mystical vortexes, relaxing at a luxurious spa, or exploring meditation and healing centers, Sedona offers a wealth of spiritual and wellness experiences. This chapter explores the key spiritual and healing locations you can visit during your stay.

Exploring Sedona's Vortexes

Sedona's vortexes are believed to be centers of heightened spiritual energy, making them popular spots for meditation, reflection, and personal healing. These natural sites are said to radiate powerful energy that can help individuals find clarity, balance, and peace. Here are some of Sedona's most well-known vortexes:

1. Cathedral Rock Vortex

Highlights:
The **Cathedral Rock Vortex** is one of Sedona's most iconic spiritual spots, known for its strong masculine energy that promotes mental clarity, inner strength, and decisive action. Located along the Cathedral Rock hiking trail, visitors can meditate in this vortex while surrounded by stunning red rock formations. It's a perfect spot for spiritual seekers, meditators, and anyone looking to experience the beauty and energy of Sedona.

Pricing:
A **Red Rock Pass** is required for parking:

- $5 for a day pass
- $15 for a weekly pass
- $20 for an annual pass

Location:
Cathedral Rock, Back O' Beyond Road, Sedona, AZ 86336
Trailhead Map

2. Bell Rock Vortex

Highlights:
Located near Oak Creek Village, **Bell Rock** is another renowned Sedona vortex, believed to offer a balance of masculine and feminine energies. Visitors come here to meditate, hike, and experience the grounding energy that is said to bring harmony and balance. Bell Rock is also a popular hiking area with trails that provide stunning views of the surrounding red rocks, making it an ideal destination for those looking to combine nature with spiritual reflection.

Pricing:
A **Red Rock Pass** is required for parking:

- $5 for a day pass
- $15 for a weekly pass
- $20 for an annual pass

Location:
Bell Rock Trailhead, Sedona, AZ 86336
Map & Directions

3. Airport Mesa Vortex

Highlights:
The **Airport Mesa Vortex** is one of Sedona's most accessible vortexes and offers an uplifting energy that's said to inspire creativity and insight. Located just off Airport Road, this spot is also known for its panoramic views of Sedona's red rocks, making it a popular location for sunset meditation and spiritual reflection.

Pricing:
Parking fee: $3 per vehicle.

Location:
Sedona Airport Scenic Lookout, Airport Road, Sedona, AZ 86336
Map & Directions

4. Boynton Canyon Vortex

Highlights:
The **Boynton Canyon Vortex** offers a peaceful, balanced energy, combining both masculine and feminine forces. It's a perfect spot for meditation and healing, with visitors often describing the experience as calming and rejuvenating. The vortex is located along the Boynton Canyon Trail, which leads hikers through a serene red rock canyon and past the Kachina Woman rock formation.

Pricing:
A **Red Rock Pass** is required for parking:

- $5 for a day pass
- $15 for a weekly pass
- $20 for an annual pass

Location:
Boynton Canyon Trail, Boynton Pass Road, Sedona, AZ 86336
Map & Directions

Wellness Retreats and Spas

Sedona's calming surroundings and spiritual energy make it an ideal location for wellness retreats and spa experiences. Visitors come to rejuvenate their bodies and minds through a variety of healing treatments, from massages and facials to energy work and meditation. Whether you're looking for a quick spa day or an immersive retreat, Sedona offers options for every type of wellness seeker.

1. Mii amo Spa at Enchantment Resort

Highlights:
Located in Boynton Canyon, **Mii amo** is a luxury destination spa known for its beautiful setting and exceptional wellness services. Guests can choose from a wide range of treatments, including massages, facials, body wraps, and energy healing. Mii amo's "Journey" packages offer multi-day retreats focused on relaxation,

personal growth, and spiritual renewal. Daily yoga, meditation, and access to wellness workshops are also available.

Pricing:

- Day spa access starts at $135 per person.
- "Journey" packages range from $2,000 to $5,000 depending on length and services.

Location:
525 Boynton Canyon Rd, Sedona, AZ 86336
Map & Directions

Website:
https://www.miiamo.com

2. Sedona Rouge Resort & Spa

Highlights:
Sedona Rouge Spa offers a luxurious and relaxing atmosphere with a range of services designed to refresh the mind and body. Signature treatments include aromatherapy, hot stone therapy, and detoxifying body wraps. The spa also provides energy healing sessions, Reiki, and acupuncture. Sedona Rouge's peaceful environment makes it a great choice for unwinding after a day of hiking or exploring Sedona's spiritual sites.

Pricing:

- Treatments range from $125 to $300.
- Custom spa packages and retreats are available.

Location:
2250 W State Route 89A, Sedona, AZ 86336
Map & Directions

3. Amara Resort & Spa

Highlights:

Situated along Oak Creek, **Amara Resort & Spa** offers a tranquil spa experience in a stunning natural setting. The spa offers a variety of treatments, including massages, facials, and body scrubs, with a focus on relaxation and healing. One of their signature treatments, the Rain Dance Massage, incorporates Native American healing practices and essential oils. Guests can also participate in yoga classes, meditation, and enjoy the spa's outdoor hot tubs and saltwater infinity pool with views of the red rocks.

Pricing:

- Spa services range from $150 to $250.
- Custom spa packages and retreats are also available.

Location:

100 Amara Ln, Sedona, AZ 86336
Map & Directions

Meditation and Healing Centers

Sedona's peaceful atmosphere and spiritual energy have made it a hub for meditation and healing centers. Whether you're new to meditation or looking to deepen your spiritual practice, Sedona offers a variety of centers that focus on mindfulness, energy healing, and personal growth.

1. Sedona Meditation Center

Highlights:

The **Sedona Meditation Center** offers classes and workshops that help visitors connect with their inner selves through meditation, self-awareness practices, and spiritual healing. Daily meditation sessions are available, as well as workshops on chakra balancing, mindfulness, and energy healing. The center provides a peaceful, supportive environment for anyone seeking personal growth or spiritual renewal.

Pricing:

- Group meditation classes start at $20.
- Private sessions range from $75 to $150.

Location:
340 Jordan Rd, Sedona, AZ 86336
Map & Directions

Website:
https://www.sedonameditationcenter.org

2. Sedona Soul Adventures

Highlights:
Sedona Soul Adventures offers fully customized spiritual retreats designed to promote healing, personal transformation, and spiritual growth. The retreats are tailored to individual needs and include a combination of energy work, spiritual counseling, meditation, and yoga. Themes range from emotional healing to spiritual awakening, with participants receiving personalized guidance throughout the retreat.

Pricing:

- Custom retreats start at $2,495 for three days.
- Multi-day retreats range from $3,000 to $8,000 depending on length and services.

Location:
120 Canyon Cir Dr, Sedona, AZ 86351
Map & Directions

Website:
https://sedonasouladventures.com

3. SpiritQuest Sedona Retreats

Highlights:
SpiritQuest specializes in wellness retreats focused on healing, spiritual growth, and emotional balance. Retreats include energy work, Reiki, sound healing, and sacred ceremonies, all aimed at promoting personal transformation. Whether you're

seeking physical rejuvenation or spiritual awakening, SpiritQuest offers a nurturing space to explore your inner journey and find balance.

Pricing:

- One-day retreats start at $695.
- Multi-day retreats range from $1,500 to $4,000 depending on the services included.

Location:
75 Kallof Pl, Sedona, AZ 86336
Map & Directions

Website:
https://retreatsinsedona.com

Sedona's Red Rock Formations

Sedona's striking red rock formations are among the most recognizable landscapes in the American Southwest. These towering, vividly colored structures have long fascinated geologists, photographers, and nature enthusiasts. Beyond their stunning beauty, the red rocks hold a rich geological history. For visitors curious about the science behind these formations and those seeking to capture their beauty in photographs, Sedona offers a variety of locations to explore. This chapter discusses the formation of Sedona's red rocks and highlights the best spots for photography, ensuring visitors can fully appreciate and document the magnificence of these natural wonders.

The Science Behind the Red Rocks

The vibrant red rocks that define Sedona's landscape were shaped over millions of years through sedimentation, tectonic movement, and erosion. The iconic red color comes from iron oxide, or hematite, embedded in the rock, which gives the sandstone its unique hue.

Geological History of Sedona's Red Rocks

Sedona's red rock formations are primarily composed of **Schnebly Hill Sandstone**, formed over 275 million years ago during the Permian period. During this era, the region was covered by vast deserts and shallow seas, which deposited layers of sand and minerals that eventually compressed into rock. The red color of these formations comes from iron that oxidized over time, much like rust.

As tectonic forces uplifted the land, these sandstone layers were exposed to the elements. Wind and water erosion sculpted the rock into the spires, mesas, and buttes that we see today. Iconic formations like **Cathedral Rock**, **Bell Rock**, and **Courthouse Butte** are all part of this fascinating geological process.

Iron Oxide and Sedona's Red Color

The red hue of Sedona's rocks is due to the presence of iron oxide particles in the sandstone, which oxidized and gave the rock its deep red color. The red color is most prominent in the upper layers of the rock, with deeper layers displaying orange or white tones due to the lower concentration of iron oxide.

Sedona's red rocks are also known for their ability to change colors throughout the day. Depending on the position of the sun, the rocks can appear bright red in the morning, orange in the afternoon, and deep purple at sunset, offering a dynamic visual experience.

Best Spots for Photography

Sedona's red rock formations offer endless opportunities for photography, whether you're a professional or simply a visitor looking to capture the stunning beauty of the landscape. Here are some of the best locations to photograph Sedona's red rocks:

1. Cathedral Rock

Highlights:
One of the most photographed locations in Sedona, **Cathedral Rock** offers breathtaking views and photo opportunities from various angles. The tall spires and scenic backdrop make it a favorite among photographers, especially at sunset when the rocks are illuminated by a golden glow. Another popular photo spot is the reflection of Cathedral Rock in the waters of Oak Creek at **Red Rock Crossing**, which creates a serene and picturesque scene.

Best Time for Photography:

- Sunset and late afternoon for warm lighting.
- Sunrise for softer lighting and fewer crowds.

Pricing:
A **Red Rock Pass** is required for parking:

- $5 for a day pass
- $15 for a weekly pass
- $20 for an annual pass

Location:
Back O' Beyond Road, Sedona, AZ 86336
Trailhead Map

2. Bell Rock

Highlights:
Bell Rock is another iconic formation and a fantastic location for photography, particularly with its unique bell-shaped silhouette. The surrounding area offers several viewpoints, making it a great spot for panoramic shots of the red rock landscape. The **Bell Rock Pathway** provides easy access to various viewpoints where you can capture Bell Rock against the backdrop of Sedona's rugged beauty.

Best Time for Photography:

- Sunrise and early morning for soft lighting and fewer visitors.
- Late afternoon and sunset for warm, dramatic tones.

Pricing:
A **Red Rock Pass** is required for parking:

- $5 for a day pass
- $15 for a weekly pass
- $20 for an annual pass

Location:
Bell Rock Trailhead, Sedona, AZ 86336
Map & Directions

3. Airport Mesa Overlook

Highlights:
The **Airport Mesa Overlook** offers one of the best panoramic views of Sedona's red rock formations. From this elevated viewpoint, photographers can capture sweeping views of **Cathedral Rock**, **Bell Rock**, **Courthouse Butte**, and other formations. This location is particularly popular at sunset, when the golden light enhances the red rock formations, making them glow. It's an ideal spot for wide-angle shots and dramatic landscape photography.

Best Time for Photography:

- Sunset for golden hour lighting and expansive views.
- Early morning for clearer skies and fewer crowds.

Pricing:
Parking fee: $3 per vehicle.

Location:
Airport Road, Sedona, AZ 86336
Map & Directions

4. Devil's Bridge

Highlights:
Devil's Bridge is a natural sandstone arch that offers an exciting photography opportunity for adventurers. The bridge's large size and unique shape make it a popular spot for photos, and the hike up to the bridge provides several stunning viewpoints. Once at the top, you can capture incredible shots of the bridge and the surrounding landscape. Brave photographers can walk across the bridge for a truly unique perspective.

Best Time for Photography:

- Early morning to avoid crowds and capture soft lighting.
- Mid-morning or afternoon for bright, clear shots of the bridge and surroundings.

Pricing:
A **Red Rock Pass** is required for parking:

- $5 for a day pass
- $15 for a weekly pass
- $20 for an annual pass

Location:
Dry Creek Road, Sedona, AZ 86336
Trailhead Map

5. Schnebly Hill Road

Highlights:
For a more rugged and less-traveled photography experience, **Schnebly Hill Road** offers dramatic views of Sedona's red rock formations as the road winds through canyons and forests. The road has several scenic pull-offs where you can stop to capture the landscape. Elevated vantage points along Schnebly Hill Road offer sweeping panoramic views, making it a perfect spot for wide-angle shots of the red rocks.

Best Time for Photography:

- Sunrise or late afternoon for the best lighting.
- Cloudy days provide diffused light for softer images.

Pricing:
Free access, though a high-clearance vehicle is recommended for navigating the road.

Location:
Schnebly Hill Road, Sedona, AZ 86336
Map & Directions

Tips for Photographing Sedona's Red Rocks

1. **Golden Hour**: The best time to photograph Sedona's red rocks is during the golden hours—shortly after sunrise and just before sunset. The soft, warm light during these times makes the rocks glow in brilliant red-orange tones.
2. **Wide-Angle Lens**: A wide-angle lens is ideal for capturing the grandeur of Sedona's landscape. Many of the formations are expansive, so a wide lens will allow you to frame more of the scenery.

3. **Polarizing Filter**: A polarizing filter can help enhance the contrast between the red rocks and the sky, creating vibrant, high-contrast images. It can also reduce glare when photographing near water or reflective surfaces.
4. **Framing with Nature**: Use nearby trees, cacti, or rock formations to frame your shots, adding depth and interest to your compositions.
5. **Early Mornings**: Visiting popular photography spots early in the morning helps avoid crowds and ensures you can take your time setting up shots.

Art and Culture in Sedona

Sedona is renowned for its thriving art and cultural scene, attracting artists, collectors, and art enthusiasts alike. The area's stunning natural beauty has inspired generations of creatives, whose works often reflect the vibrant landscapes, local cultures, and spiritual energy that define Sedona. From art galleries and museums to cultural festivals and artisan shopping, Sedona offers a wide range of opportunities to explore its artistic offerings. This chapter highlights some of the top cultural attractions, including the famed **Tlaquepaque Arts & Shopping Village**, the town's standout galleries and museums, and its lively art festivals.

Tlaquepaque Arts & Shopping Village

Highlights:

Tlaquepaque Arts & Shopping Village is a landmark in Sedona's art scene, designed to resemble a traditional Mexican village with cobblestone streets, charming courtyards, and beautiful fountains. Established in the 1970s, this art and shopping destination houses over 45 galleries, specialty shops, and studios, featuring everything from fine art and sculptures to jewelry, ceramics, and textiles.

Tlaquepaque offers more than just shopping—it's a cultural experience. The galleries and shops display works by local artisans and internationally known artists, providing visitors with a diverse range of art to explore. In addition, the village regularly hosts art shows, live music, and festivals, making it a hub of cultural activity in Sedona. Popular galleries like **Rowe Fine Art Gallery** and **Kuivato Glass Art Gallery** feature contemporary Southwest art and stunning glasswork, while **Turquoise Tortoise Gallery** showcases handcrafted jewelry and pottery inspired by Native American heritage.

Pricing:
Entrance to Tlaquepaque is free, though prices for art and items vary by gallery and shop.

Location:
336 State Route 179, Sedona, AZ 86336
Map & Directions

Website:
https://www.tlaq.com

Sedona Art Galleries and Museums

Sedona is home to numerous art galleries and museums that showcase a broad array of artistic styles and mediums. Whether you're interested in contemporary works, local crafts, or Native American art, Sedona's galleries offer something for every art lover. Below are some must-visit galleries and museums in the area:

1. Sedona Arts Center

Highlights:
Founded in 1958, the **Sedona Arts Center** is one of Sedona's oldest cultural institutions, providing a platform for both established and emerging artists to exhibit their work. The center features rotating exhibits across different styles and mediums, including painting, sculpture, photography, and mixed media. It also offers art workshops, classes, and cultural events throughout the year.

The **Fine Art Gallery** at the Sedona Arts Center showcases pieces from over 100 local artists, including ceramics, paintings, jewelry, and more, all available for purchase.

Pricing:
Free gallery entry; prices vary for workshops and classes.

Location:
15 Art Barn Rd, Sedona, AZ 86336
Map & Directions

Website:
https://sedonaartscenter.org

2. Exposures International Gallery of Fine Art

Highlights:
Exposures International is one of the largest and most prestigious art galleries in Sedona, showcasing an extensive collection of fine art, including paintings, sculptures, jewelry, and glasswork. The gallery highlights contemporary works from artists around the world, as well as local pieces that capture Sedona's breathtaking landscapes.

Exposures International also features an impressive outdoor sculpture garden, making it a must-see for both art collectors and casual visitors alike.

Pricing:
Free entry; art prices vary widely depending on the piece.

Location:
561 State Route 179, Sedona, AZ 86336
Map & Directions

Website:
https://www.exposuresfineart.com

3. The Museum of Northern Arizona

Highlights:
While located in nearby Flagstaff, the **Museum of Northern Arizona** offers valuable insight into the region's art, culture, and history. The museum's collection includes Native American pottery, textiles, jewelry, and paintings, highlighting the artistic traditions of the Colorado Plateau. The museum also features rotating exhibits that

showcase contemporary Native American art, environmental themes, and local history.

This museum is an excellent destination for those interested in exploring the cultural heritage of the region, beyond Sedona's local art scene.

Pricing:

- $12 for adults
- $8 for youth (10-17)
- Free for children under 10

Location:
3101 N Fort Valley Rd, Flagstaff, AZ 86001
Map & Directions

Website:
https://musnaz.org

Local Art Festivals

Sedona's vibrant artistic community comes to life through several annual art festivals that showcase the work of local and national artists. These events are a great way for visitors to immerse themselves in the town's creative spirit while enjoying live performances, demonstrations, and workshops. Below are some of Sedona's most popular art festivals:

1. Sedona Arts Festival

Highlights:
The **Sedona Arts Festival** is one of the area's premier art events, held every October. It brings together over 100 artists from across the country, offering a wide range of artwork, including paintings, sculpture, jewelry, ceramics, and photography. The festival also features live music, art demonstrations, and a **KidZone** with interactive art activities for children. Visitors can also explore the **Gourmet Gallery**, which showcases local chefs and food vendors.

Pricing:

- $10 for adults (online)
- Free for children under 12

Location:
995 Upper Red Rock Loop Rd, Sedona, AZ 86336
Map & Directions

Website:
https://sedonaartsfestival.org

2. Plein Air Festival

Highlights:
The **Sedona Plein Air Festival** celebrates the art of painting outdoors, attracting top plein air artists who create their works in real-time amidst Sedona's stunning landscapes. Held annually in October, the festival offers visitors a chance to watch artists at work in iconic Sedona locations. The event includes painting demonstrations, workshops, and an art exhibition where the finished works are displayed and sold.

Pricing:
Free to attend; artwork prices vary.

Location:
Various locations throughout Sedona (check the website for details).

Website:https://sedonapleinairfestival.org

3. Tlaquepaque Festival of Lights

Highlights:
The **Tlaquepaque Festival of Lights** is a festive event held in December that transforms the Tlaquepaque Arts & Shopping Village into a magical holiday scene. Over 6,000 luminarias light up the village's pathways, while visitors can enjoy live music, performances, and carolers. The event is perfect for families and offers a chance to shop for unique holiday gifts while experiencing Sedona's art and culture in a festive atmosphere.

Pricing:
Free to attend.

Location:
336 State Route 179, Sedona, AZ 86336
Map & Directions

Website:
https://www.tlaq.com

Sedona for Adventure Seekers

Sedona's stunning red rock landscapes and diverse natural surroundings make it an ideal destination for adventure lovers. Whether you're looking to float above the desert in a hot air balloon, explore rugged terrain on horseback, or enjoy the thrill of a helicopter tour, Sedona offers plenty of exciting activities that showcase its natural beauty. This section highlights some of the best adventurous activities in Sedona, including hot air balloon rides, helicopter tours, and horseback riding, with information on the experiences, prices, and locations.

Hot Air Balloon Rides

Highlights:

A **hot air balloon ride** is one of the most magical ways to take in Sedona's breathtaking landscapes. As you ascend into the sky, you'll be treated to panoramic views of Sedona's red rock formations, expansive deserts, and lush green valleys. Most hot air balloon rides take place at sunrise, offering a peaceful flight as the first rays of light illuminate the red rocks, casting them in warm hues of red, orange, and pink.

These rides generally last 3-4 hours, including transportation, pre-flight preparation, and the balloon flight, which typically takes about 1 to 1.5 hours. The experience often ends with a post-flight celebration featuring champagne and light refreshments. During the flight, you'll have an unmatched view of famous landmarks like **Cathedral Rock**, **Bell Rock**, and the **Verde Valley**, making it a memorable adventure.

Pricing:

- Prices range from $250 to $350 per person, depending on the operator and package.

Recommended Operators:

- **Red Rock Balloon Adventures**
  https://redrockballoons.com
  Location: 105 Canyon Diablo Rd, Sedona, AZ 86351

- **Northern Light Balloon Expeditions**
  https://www.northernlightballoons.com
  Location: Sedona, AZ 86336

Best Time for the Experience:

- Hot air balloon rides are usually offered early in the morning to take advantage of calm winds and ideal sunrise lighting. They are available year-round, with spring and fall being the most popular times due to the pleasant weather.

Helicopter Tours

Highlights:

For those seeking a more adrenaline-filled adventure, **helicopter tours** over Sedona's red rocks provide a thrilling way to experience the area's stunning beauty. Helicopter tours give you access to remote areas and offer an up-close view of iconic rock formations such as **Cathedral Rock**, **Bell Rock**, **Chimney Rock**, and the **Secret Canyon**.

One of the key benefits of a helicopter tour is the ability to fly over difficult-to-reach places, including **Coconino National Forest** and **Oak Creek Canyon**. Depending on the tour, you can enjoy flights lasting from 20 minutes to an hour, giving you the chance to take in Sedona's incredible landscapes from a unique perspective and capture incredible photos.

Pricing:

- Short tours (15-20 minutes) range from $170 to $250 per person.
- Longer tours (30-60 minutes) range from $350 to $600 per person.

Recommended Operators:

- **Sedona Air Tours**
  https://www.sedonaairtours.com
  Location: 1225 Airport Rd, Sedona, AZ 86336

- **Guidance Air**
  https://www.guidanceair.com
  Location: 1200 Airport Rd, Sedona, AZ 86336

Best Time for the Experience:

- Helicopter tours operate year-round, with mornings and late afternoons offering the best light for photography and the most striking views of the red rocks.

Horseback Riding

Highlights:

Horseback riding is a fantastic way to explore Sedona's landscapes while connecting with nature. Riding through the region's rugged trails allows you to experience the desert, forests, and canyons in an immersive way. Guided horseback tours take riders through areas like **Coconino National Forest**, **Dead Horse Ranch State Park**, and along **Oak Creek**, offering spectacular views of Sedona's red rocks and the surrounding wilderness.

Suitable for all levels, from beginners to experienced riders, these tours often follow trails that lead through diverse environments, such as the **Munds Mountain Wilderness** and **Red Rock State Park**. Some tours also include opportunities for picnics or exploring historical landmarks along the way. Sunset and evening rides are especially popular, allowing riders to witness Sedona's red rocks at their most beautiful as the day comes to a close.

Pricing:

- One- to two-hour rides range from $75 to $150 per person.
- Half-day and full-day rides range from $200 to $350 per person, depending on the length and itinerary.

Recommended Operators:

- **M Diamond Ranch**
  https://www.mdiamondranch.com
  Location: 2717 W State Route 89A, Sedona, AZ 86336

- **Horsin' Around Adventures**
  https://horsinaroundadventures.com
  Location: 75 N Viejo Dr, Cornville, AZ 86325

Best Time for the Experience:

- Horseback rides are available throughout the year, though spring and fall provide the best weather. Sunset rides are particularly recommended for their stunning scenery and beautiful light.

Tips for Adventure Seekers in Sedona

1. **Book in Advance**: Adventure activities like hot air balloon rides and helicopter tours are in high demand, especially during peak seasons (spring and fall), so booking ahead is essential.
2. **Dress Appropriately**: Wear comfortable clothing and closed-toe shoes. Be prepared for temperature fluctuations, especially in the morning or evening, by dressing in layers.
3. **Stay Hydrated**: Sedona's dry desert climate can lead to dehydration, so it's important to bring plenty of water, especially for horseback rides or outdoor excursions.
4. **Capture the Moment**: Bring a camera or smartphone to capture the incredible views you'll encounter during your adventures, whether from the sky, on horseback, or hiking trails.
5. **Respect Nature**: Always stick to designated trails and avoid disturbing wildlife or the natural environment. Sedona's landscapes are delicate, so it's important to leave no trace.

Sedona's Hidden Gems

While Sedona is famous for its iconic red rock formations and popular attractions, it also offers a variety of hidden treasures for those seeking solitude and a quieter experience. From secret hiking trails to peaceful lookout points and lesser-known vortex sites, these hidden gems allow visitors to enjoy Sedona's natural beauty without the crowds. In this chapter, we'll explore some of Sedona's best-kept secrets, including secluded hiking spots, tranquil vistas, and off-the-radar vortex locations, perfect for adventurers looking to connect with the area on a deeper level.

Secret Hiking Spots

For those who prefer exploring in peace, Sedona has several hidden hiking trails that provide quiet beauty, spectacular views, and a closer connection to nature. These trails are lesser-known but no less stunning than the more popular ones.

1. Bear Mountain Trail

Highlights:

Bear Mountain Trail is a challenging but rewarding hike that offers some of the best panoramic views in Sedona. Despite its stunning vistas, this trail is often overlooked, making it a peaceful escape for hikers seeking solitude. The trail covers roughly 5 miles round trip and is known for its steep, rocky terrain and multiple elevation gains. The hike culminates in a breathtaking 360-degree view of Sedona, the Verde Valley, and the San Francisco Peaks in the distance, making it well worth the effort.

Ideal for experienced hikers, Bear Mountain offers serenity and awe-inspiring landscapes along a trail less traveled by the majority of visitors.

Pricing:

A **Red Rock Pass** is required for parking:

- $5 for a day pass
- $15 for a weekly pass
- $20 for an annual pass

Location:

Bear Mountain Trailhead, Boynton Pass Rd, Sedona, AZ 86336
Trailhead Map

2. Soldier Pass Cave Trail

Highlights:

While **Soldier Pass Trail** is popular, the hidden **Soldier Pass Cave** is an undiscovered gem along this route. This offshoot of the main trail leads to a secluded cave with stunning rock formations and a unique atmosphere. The cave is tucked away and requires some effort to find, but the reward is a serene, uncrowded spot perfect for exploration and photography. Natural sunlight streams into the cave through an opening in the ceiling, creating a mystical, illuminated space.

The entire hike, including the cave, is about 4.5 miles round trip and offers a peaceful experience for those willing to venture off the main path.

Pricing:

A **Red Rock Pass** is required for parking:

- $5 for a day pass
- $15 for a weekly pass
- $20 for an annual pass

Location:

Soldier Pass Trailhead, Forest Service Rd, Sedona, AZ 86336
Trailhead Map

3. Wilson Mountain Trail

Highlights:

For a longer, more remote hiking experience, the **Wilson Mountain Trail** takes hikers to the highest point in Sedona. This 11-mile round-trip hike is known for its rugged terrain and significant elevation gain, but the panoramic views from the top are worth every step. From the summit, hikers can see the Verde Valley, the Mogollon Rim, and Sedona's red rock formations in stunning detail.

Despite being one of the most rewarding hikes in Sedona, Wilson Mountain is less traveled, offering a tranquil escape from busier trails. The views from the summit are particularly breathtaking during fall, when the trees lining the trail are ablaze with color.

Pricing:

A **Red Rock Pass** is required for parking:

- $5 for a day pass
- $15 for a weekly pass
- $20 for an annual pass

Location:

Midgley Bridge Picnic Area, Sedona, AZ 86336
Trailhead Map

Quiet Lookout Points

If you're looking for serene, panoramic views without the hustle and bustle, Sedona has several hidden lookout points that offer peaceful environments to enjoy the natural beauty.

1. Schnebly Hill Vista

Highlights:
Schnebly Hill Vista is one of Sedona's lesser-known yet most stunning viewpoints. Accessible via a rugged dirt road (a high-clearance vehicle is recommended), this overlook offers expansive views of Sedona's red rocks and the Verde Valley. It's a perfect spot for sunrise or sunset photography and provides a peaceful, quiet setting away from more popular viewpoints.

Though the road to Schnebly Hill Vista can be challenging, the serene views and seclusion make it an ideal spot for those looking to escape the crowds.

Pricing:
Free access, though a high-clearance vehicle is recommended.

Location:
Schnebly Hill Rd, Sedona, AZ 86336
Map & Directions

2. Merry-Go-Round Rock

Highlights:

Tucked away along Schnebly Hill Road, **Merry-Go-Round Rock** is a hidden gem that offers incredible views of Sedona's red rock canyons and forests. This quiet spot is ideal for a peaceful picnic or to capture stunning photographs of the surrounding landscape. The rock's remote location makes it a great escape from the busier areas, offering a tranquil atmosphere.

Accessible by hiking or driving (with a high-clearance vehicle), Merry-Go-Round Rock is one of Sedona's best-kept secrets for adventure seekers who want to enjoy the area's beauty without the crowds.

Pricing:

Free access, though a high-clearance vehicle is recommended.

Location:

Schnebly Hill Rd, Sedona, AZ 86336
Map & Directions

Hidden Vortex Locations

While many visitors flock to well-known vortex sites like Bell Rock and Cathedral Rock, there are also hidden vortex locations that offer a quieter and more personal experience of Sedona's energy. These lesser-known vortexes provide an intimate setting for meditation and reflection, away from the more crowded areas.

1. Boynton Canyon Vortex (Away from the Crowds)

Highlights:
The **Boynton Canyon Vortex** is one of Sedona's famous energy sites, but there are quieter spots within the canyon where you can experience the vortex energy without the crowds. As you venture further into the canyon along the trail, you'll find secluded areas that still hold the spiritual energy of the vortex, providing a peaceful environment for meditation and reflection.

Boynton Canyon is also home to stunning red rock formations and lush vegetation, making it a hidden gem for those looking to experience both natural beauty and spiritual energy in a more tranquil setting.

Pricing:
A **Red Rock Pass** is required for parking:

- $5 for a day pass
- $15 for a weekly pass
- $20 for an annual pass

Location:
Boynton Canyon Trailhead, Boynton Pass Rd, Sedona, AZ 86336
Trailhead Map

2. The Kachina Woman Vortex

Highlights:
Located in Boynton Canyon, the **Kachina Woman Vortex** is a lesser-known vortex spot near the distinctive Kachina Woman rock formation. Believed to hold powerful feminine energy, this vortex site is perfect for quiet meditation and reflection. Its

remote location means you're likely to have the space to yourself, making it an ideal spot for spiritual practices.

The hike to the Kachina Woman Vortex also offers spectacular views of the canyon, and its relatively hidden status makes it a special place for those looking for a more private vortex experience.

Pricing:
A **Red Rock Pass** is required for parking:

- $5 for a day pass
- $15 for a weekly pass
- $20 for an annual pass

Location:
Boynton Canyon Trail, Sedona, AZ 86336
Trailhead Map

Day Trips from Sedona

Sedona's prime location in northern Arizona makes it the perfect starting point for exploring nearby towns, attractions, and natural landmarks. Whether you want to discover the charm of historic towns, hike through scenic canyons, or marvel at the majestic Grand Canyon, day trips from Sedona offer a variety of exciting adventures. This section covers some of the best day trips from Sedona, including visits to nearby towns such as **Flagstaff**, **Jerome**, and **Oak Creek Canyon**, as well as an unforgettable excursion to **Grand Canyon National Park**.

Exploring Nearby Towns and Attractions

1. Flagstaff

Highlights:
About 45 minutes north of Sedona, **Flagstaff** offers a dramatic contrast to Sedona's red rock landscape. Nestled at 7,000 feet in elevation, Flagstaff is surrounded by the Coconino National Forest and the San Francisco Peaks, making it a hub for outdoor activities like hiking, skiing, and mountain biking. In addition to its outdoor appeal, Flagstaff is a lively college town known for its historic Route 66 charm, breweries, and local cafes.

Visitors can explore the **Lowell Observatory**, famous for the discovery of Pluto, or wander through Flagstaff's quaint downtown, full of shops, restaurants, and galleries. Outdoor lovers can hike in the surrounding areas, including trails to **Mount Humphreys**, Arizona's tallest peak. In winter, **Arizona Snowbowl** becomes a popular destination for skiing and snowboarding.

Pricing:

- **Lowell Observatory**: $25 for adults, $15 for children (5-17), free for children under 5.
- **Arizona Snowbowl**: Lift ticket prices vary seasonally, ranging from $40 to $150.

Location:
Flagstaff, AZ 86001 (45 miles north of Sedona)
Map & Directions

Website:
https://www.discoverflagstaff.com

2. Jerome

Highlights:
Perched on the slopes of Cleopatra Hill, **Jerome** is a former mining town turned artist community, about 30 miles southwest of Sedona. Once called the "Wickedest Town in the West" due to its raucous mining days, Jerome is now a charming destination filled with art galleries, boutique shops, and historic sites. Visitors can learn about its colorful history at the **Jerome State Historic Park** or the **Mine Museum**, or enjoy panoramic views of the Verde Valley from its steep streets.

Jerome is also known for its haunted history, and ghost tours are a popular attraction. The **Jerome Grand Hotel**, once a hospital, is considered one of the most haunted places in the U.S. Art lovers will appreciate the town's galleries, while wine enthusiasts can enjoy tastings at local wineries.

Pricing:

- **Jerome State Historic Park**: $7 for adults, $4 for youth (7-13), free for children under 7.
- **Ghost Tours**: Prices vary by tour, with an average cost of around $30 per person.

Location:
Jerome, AZ 86331 (30 miles southwest of Sedona)
Map & Directions

Website:
https://jeromechamber.com

3. Oak Creek Canyon

Highlights:
Just a short drive north of Sedona, **Oak Creek Canyon** is one of Arizona's most scenic drives and a great option for a nature-filled day trip. Known for its lush greenery, towering cliffs, and clear streams, the **Oak Creek Canyon Scenic Drive** on

Highway 89A winds through the canyon for about 14 miles, offering breathtaking viewpoints, picnic spots, and hiking trails.

A must-see stop along the route is **Slide Rock State Park**, where visitors can swim or slide down the natural rock water slides. For those who enjoy hiking, the **West Fork Trail** is a popular option, offering a peaceful walk through the canyon with several creek crossings along the way.

Pricing:

- **Slide Rock State Park**: $10 per vehicle during weekdays, $20 per vehicle on weekends and holidays.
- **West Fork Trail**: $11 per vehicle for parking.

Location:
Oak Creek Canyon, Sedona, AZ 86336 (15 miles north of Sedona)
Map & Directions

Grand Canyon National Park

Highlights:

A trip to **Grand Canyon National Park** is a must-do for anyone visiting Sedona. Located about two hours north, the Grand Canyon is one of the world's most iconic natural landmarks. Stretching over 277 miles, this massive canyon, carved by the Colorado River, offers awe-inspiring views, scenic hiking trails, and a variety of activities.

The **South Rim** is the most accessible and popular section of the park, open year-round and home to numerous viewpoints, trails, and visitor centers. Key viewpoints include **Mather Point**, **Yavapai Point**, and **Hopi Point**, all of which provide spectacular panoramic views of the canyon. Visitors can also explore **Grand Canyon Village**, known for its historic lodges, shops, and the **Grand Canyon Railway**, or walk along the **Rim Trail**, a relatively easy trail that connects several major viewpoints.

For adventurous visitors, hiking into the canyon on trails like the **Bright Angel Trail** or **South Kaibab Trail** offers a more immersive experience. Ranger-guided programs, mule rides, and helicopter tours are also available for those looking to enhance their visit.

Pricing:

- **Entrance Fee**: $35 per vehicle (valid for 7 days).
- **Grand Canyon Railway**: Ticket prices range from $67 to $226 per person, depending on class and season.
- **Helicopter Tours**: Prices range from $250 to $450 per person, depending on the tour and duration.

Location:
Grand Canyon National Park - South Rim, AZ 86023 (110 miles north of Sedona)
Map & Directions

Tips for Day Trips from Sedona

1. **Start Early**: Many of these destinations are popular with visitors, so leaving early gives you more time to explore and avoid crowds.
2. **Check Road Conditions**: Especially in winter, be sure to check road conditions for areas like Flagstaff and the Grand Canyon, which can experience snow.
3. **Bring Snacks and Water**: Some remote destinations like Oak Creek Canyon and the Grand Canyon have limited dining options, so packing snacks and water ensures you're prepared.
4. **Dress Comfortably**: Wear layers and sturdy shoes, particularly if you plan on hiking or spending time outdoors.

Where to Eat in Sedona

Sedona boasts a diverse and exciting culinary scene that complements its beautiful landscapes. Whether you're craving local Southwest dishes, gourmet meals, or plant-based options, Sedona's dining choices offer something for every palate. From upscale restaurants with stunning views to charming cafes, this chapter explores the best places to eat in Sedona, including top restaurants, vegan and vegetarian-friendly options, and the city's thriving farm-to-table movement that emphasizes fresh, local ingredients.

Best Restaurants and Local Cuisine

Sedona is home to a variety of eateries, ranging from fine dining to casual spots, with many showcasing the bold flavors of the Southwest. Here are some of the top places to experience local cuisine:

1. Mariposa Latin Inspired Grill

Highlights:
Offering sweeping views of Sedona's red rocks, **Mariposa Latin Inspired Grill** is an elegant restaurant specializing in Latin American-inspired dishes. Its menu, curated by Chef Lisa Dahl, features South American flavors in dishes like **Argentinean filet mignon**, **Peruvian scallops**, and homemade empanadas. The combination of excellent food, breathtaking views, and a thoughtfully curated wine list makes Mariposa a popular choice for special occasions.

Pricing:

- Appetizers: $15-$30
- Entrees: $35-$60

Location:
700 AZ-89A, Sedona, AZ 86336
Map & Directions

Website:
https://mariposasedona.com

2. Elote Cafe

Highlights:
Elote Cafe offers a modern take on traditional Mexican cuisine, with bold, authentic flavors and innovative twists. The menu, inspired by Chef Jeff Smedstad's travels through Mexico, features dishes such as **Pork cheeks in mole negro**, **Lamb adobo**, and the famous **Elote (Mexican street corn)**. With a lively atmosphere and excellent margaritas, it's a favorite spot for locals and tourists alike.

Pricing:

- Appetizers: $15-$20
- Entrees: $25-$40

Location:
350 Jordan Rd, Sedona, AZ 86336
Map & Directions

Website:
https://www.elotecafe.com

3. The Hudson

Highlights:
The Hudson is a modern American bistro with a relaxed atmosphere and spectacular views of Sedona's red rocks. Known for its hearty dishes like **baby back ribs**, **grilled salmon**, and **signature burgers**, The Hudson offers casual dining with excellent food and friendly service. The rooftop patio is a perfect spot to enjoy a meal with a view.

Pricing:

- Appetizers: $12-$18
- Entrees: $25-$45

Location:
671 AZ-89A, Sedona, AZ 86336
Map & Directions

Website:
https://thehudsonsedona.com

Top Picks for Vegans and Vegetarians

Sedona offers a wide variety of vegan and vegetarian-friendly options, catering to plant-based dinners with fresh, organic ingredients and creative dishes. Here are some of the best spots for vegan and vegetarian cuisine:

1. ChocolaTree Organic Eatery

Highlights:
ChocolaTree Organic Eatery is a beloved vegan and vegetarian cafe focused on organic, gluten-free, and plant-based meals. Popular dishes include the **avocado herb sandwich**, **sunflower burger**, and **coconut curry soup**. The cafe also offers house-made chocolates and raw desserts, as well as a selection of smoothies and herbal teas, all enjoyed in a peaceful garden setting.

Pricing:

- Entrees: $15-$25
- Desserts: $7-$12

Location:
1595 AZ-89A, Sedona, AZ 86336
Map & Directions

Website:
https://chocolatree.com

2. The Secret Garden Cafe

Highlights:
Located in **Tlaquepaque Arts & Shopping Village**, **The Secret Garden Cafe** is a serene spot offering a range of vegan and vegetarian options, including the **veggie hummus wrap**, **quinoa and kale salad**, and the **vegan garden bowl**. With its tranquil garden setting and fresh, organic menu, this cafe is perfect for a healthy lunch or afternoon break.

Pricing:

- Entrees: $15-$25
- Desserts: $8-$12

Location:
336 AZ-179 #F101, Sedona, AZ 86336
Map & Directions

Website:
https://www.sedonasecretgardencafe.com

3. Picazzo's Healthy Italian Kitchen

Highlights:
Picazzo's Healthy Italian Kitchen combines Italian flavors with a focus on health, offering vegan, vegetarian, and gluten-free options. Popular menu items include the **vegan pizza primavera**, **zucchini lasagna**, and **vegan Caesar salad**. Using organic, non-GMO ingredients, Picazzo's delivers delicious, plant-based versions of classic Italian dishes.

Pricing:

- Entrees: $15-$30
- Desserts: $8-$12

Location:
1855 AZ-89A, Sedona, AZ 86336
Map & Directions

Website:
https://picazzos.com

Sedona's Farm-to-Table Movement

Sedona is home to a thriving farm-to-table movement, with many restaurants focusing on fresh, locally sourced, and organic ingredients. These establishments partner with local farms to create seasonal dishes that highlight the region's natural bounty.

1. Creekside American Bistro

Highlights:
Located along Oak Creek, **Creekside American Bistro** features a seasonal, farm-to-table menu that emphasizes fresh, local produce and sustainably raised meats. Dishes like the **creekside salad** and **pistachio-crusted lamb** showcase the best of Arizona's farms. The restaurant's outdoor seating offers beautiful views of Oak Creek and Sedona's red rocks, making it an ideal spot for brunch, lunch, or dinner.

Pricing:

- Appetizers: $10-$18
- Entrees: $25-$45

Location:
251 AZ-179, Sedona, AZ 86336
Map & Directions

Website:
https://www.creeksidebistro.com

2. Mesa Grill Sedona

Highlights:
Mesa Grill Sedona, located at the Sedona Airport, offers farm-to-table Southwestern cuisine with stunning views of the red rocks. The menu emphasizes fresh, local ingredients with dishes like **chimichurri steak** and **pan-seared trout**. The restaurant's commitment to local sourcing ensures that each dish highlights the best of the region's produce and meats.

Pricing:

- Entrees: $20-$40
- Desserts: $7-$12

Location:
1185 Airport Rd, Sedona, AZ 86336
Map & Directions

Website:
https://mesagrillsedona.com

3. Local Juicery

Highlights:
Local Juicery is a health-conscious cafe specializing in organic, cold-pressed juices, smoothies, and plant-based meals. With a focus on seasonal ingredients, the cafe offers nutrient-packed options like the **acai bowl**, **rainbow salad**, and **green detox juice**. It's a great stop for those looking to enjoy fresh, locally sourced, and clean meals.

Pricing:

- Bowls: $12-$18
- Juices: $7-$10

Location:
315 AZ-89A Suite 5, Sedona, AZ 86336
Map & Directions

Website:
https://www.localjuicery.com

Where to Stay in Sedona

Sedona is a renowned destination known for its stunning landscapes and serene atmosphere, offering a variety of accommodations to suit every traveler's needs. From luxurious resorts nestled among the red rocks to budget-friendly hotels that provide easy access to Sedona's natural beauty, you can find the perfect place to stay whether you're seeking a relaxing getaway or an adventurous escape. This section covers top luxury resorts, affordable lodging options, and the best areas to stay based on your planned activities.

Luxury Resorts and Hotels

Sedona boasts several upscale resorts that offer outstanding service, premium amenities, and stunning views of the red rock formations. These luxury accommodations are perfect for travelers looking for a pampered experience with features like spas, gourmet dining, and private rooms or suites.

1. Enchantment Resort

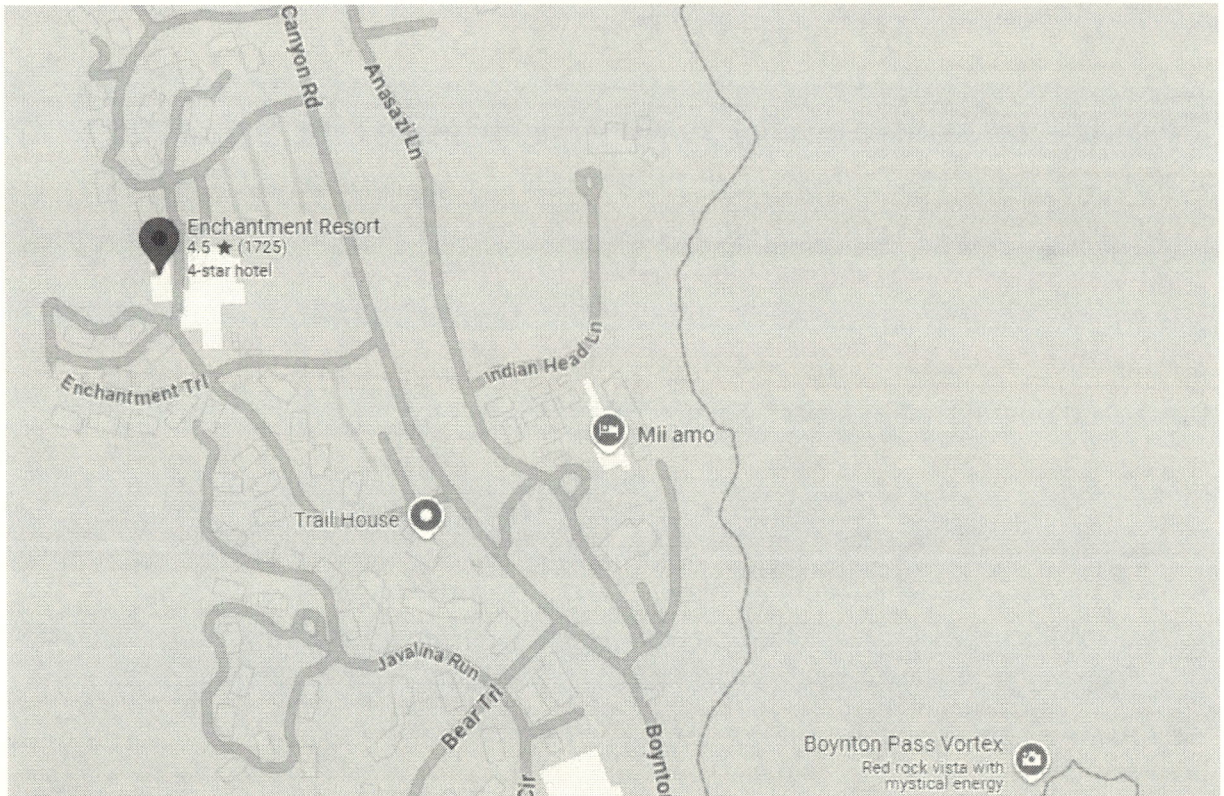

Highlights:

Situated in the heart of **Boynton Canyon**, **Enchantment Resort** is a premier luxury destination known for its spectacular views and upscale amenities. Guests can enjoy private suites or casitas, along with access to the world-renowned **Mii amo Spa**, offering holistic treatments and wellness programs. The resort also provides guided outdoor activities, such as hiking and yoga, making it an ideal spot for relaxation and adventure.

Pricing:

- Rooms range from $650 to $1,500 per night, depending on the season and type of accommodation.

Location:

525 Boynton Canyon Rd, Sedona, AZ 86336
Map & Directions

Website:

https://www.enchantmentresort.com

2. L'Auberge de Sedona

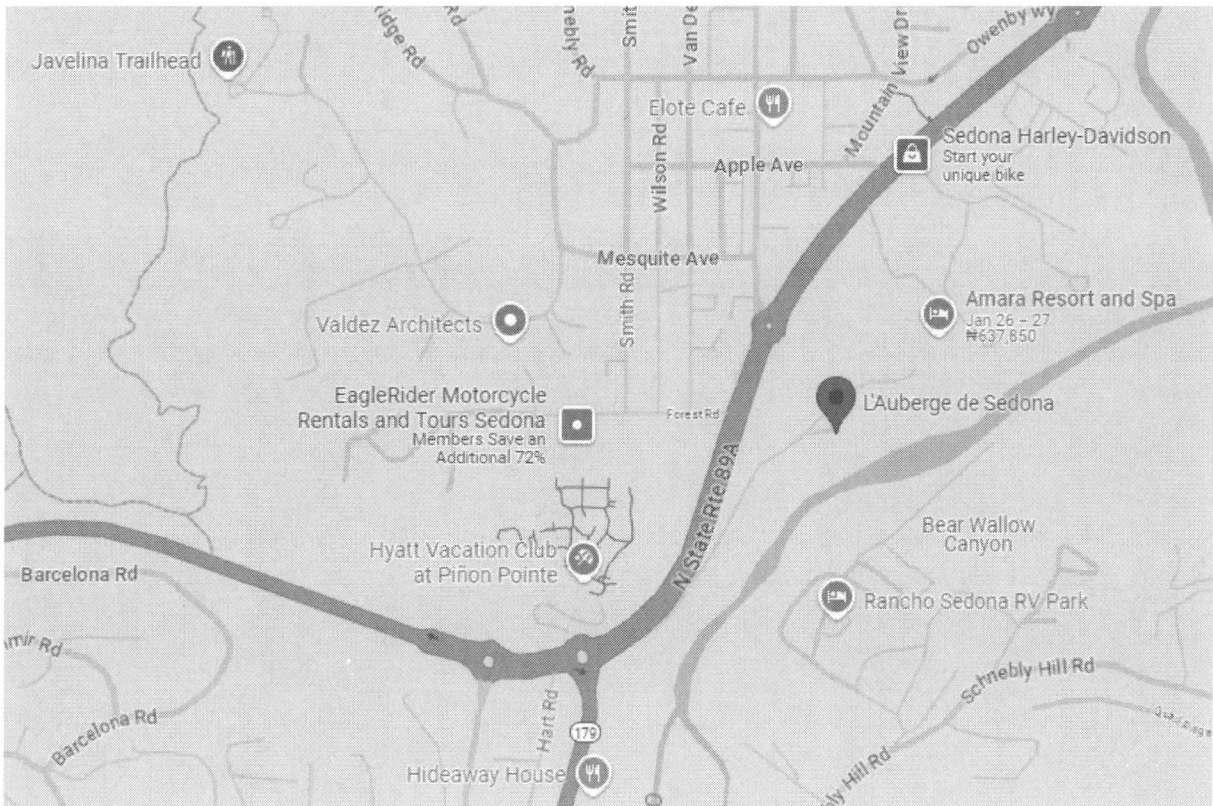

Highlights:

Located along **Oak Creek**, **L'Auberge de Sedona** offers a luxurious and tranquil retreat with charming creekside cottages and hillside rooms. The **L'Apothecary Spa** provides personalized treatments, while the **Cress on Oak Creek** restaurant offers fine dining with beautiful creek views. This resort is perfect for couples or anyone seeking a peaceful, nature-centric escape.

Pricing:

- Rooms range from $700 to $1,400 per night, depending on the season and room type.

Location:

301 Little Lane, Sedona, AZ 86336
Map & Directions

Website:

https://www.lauberge.com

3. Amara Resort and Spa

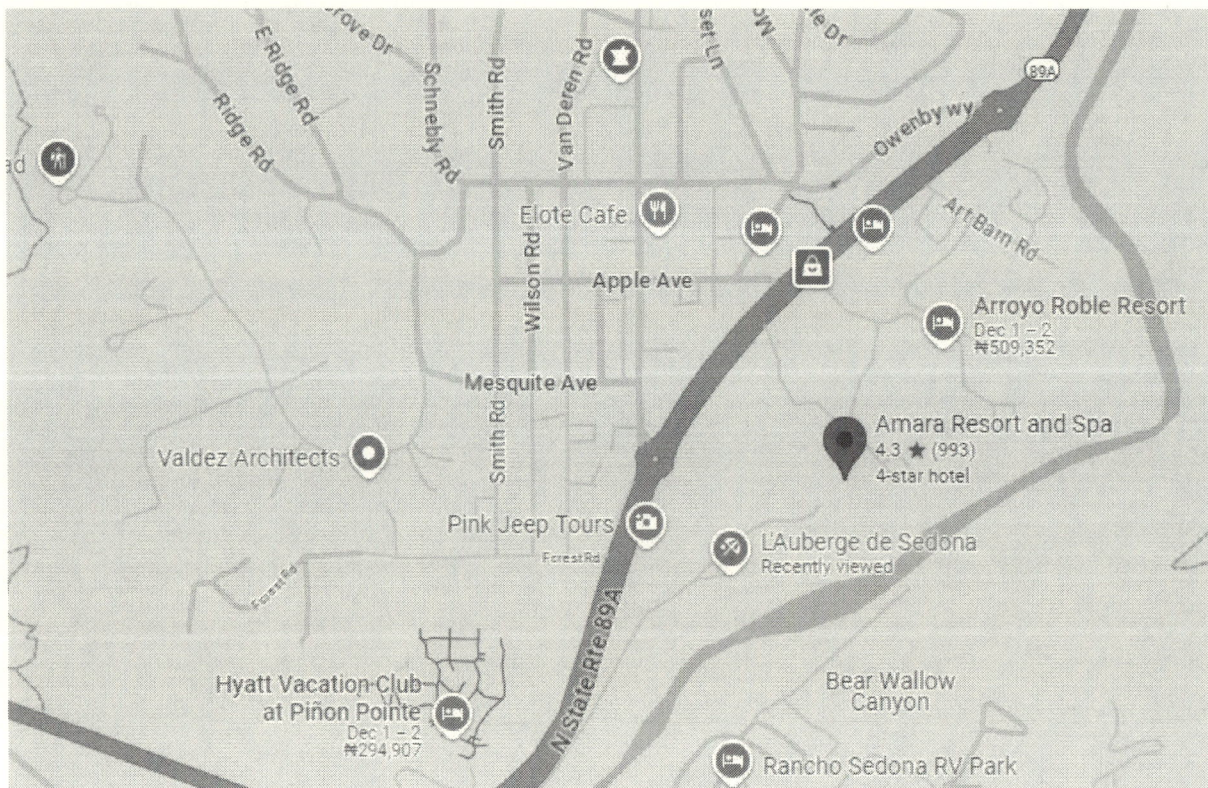

Highlights:
Set in Uptown Sedona, **Amara Resort and Spa** offers modern luxury in a laid-back atmosphere. Guests can enjoy stunning red rock views from the infinity pool, indulge in treatments at the on-site spa, or savor delicious farm-to-table cuisine at **SaltRock Southwest Kitchen**. Its central location makes it a great base for exploring Sedona's top attractions while offering a luxurious retreat.

Pricing:

- Rooms range from $400 to $850 per night, depending on the season.

Location:
100 Amara Ln, Sedona, AZ 86336
Map & Directions

Website:
https://www.amararesort.com

Budget-Friendly Accommodations

For travelers seeking more affordable accommodations, Sedona offers plenty of budget-friendly options that still provide comfort and easy access to the area's natural wonders. These hotels offer great value without sacrificing convenience.

1. Sedona Village Lodge

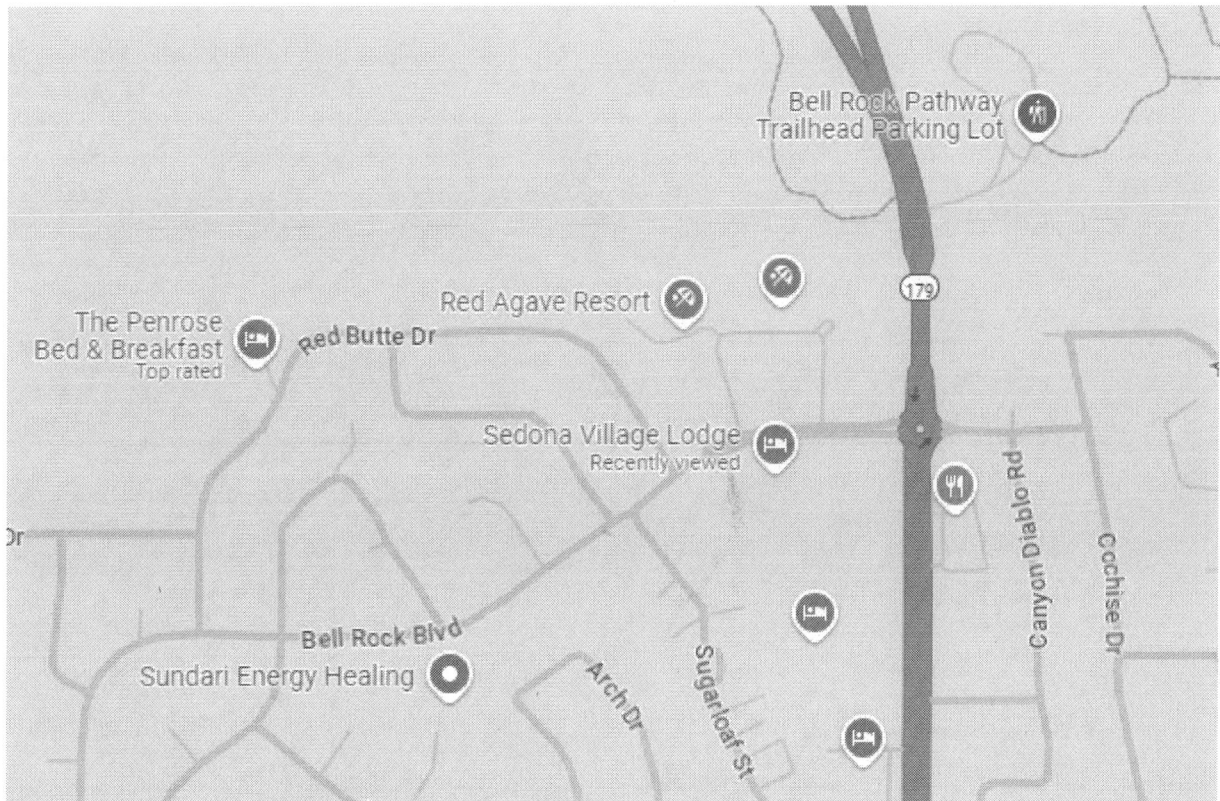

Highlights:
Located in the **Village of Oak Creek**, **Sedona Village Lodge** provides comfortable and affordable accommodations with scenic views of **Bell Rock** and **Courthouse Butte**. It's an excellent choice for budget-conscious travelers who want easy access to popular hiking trails and nearby restaurants.

Pricing:

- Rooms range from $120 to $200 per night, depending on the season.

Location:
105 Bell Rock Plaza, Sedona, AZ 86351
Map & Directions

Website:
https://www.sedonavillagelodge.com

2. Baby Quail Inn

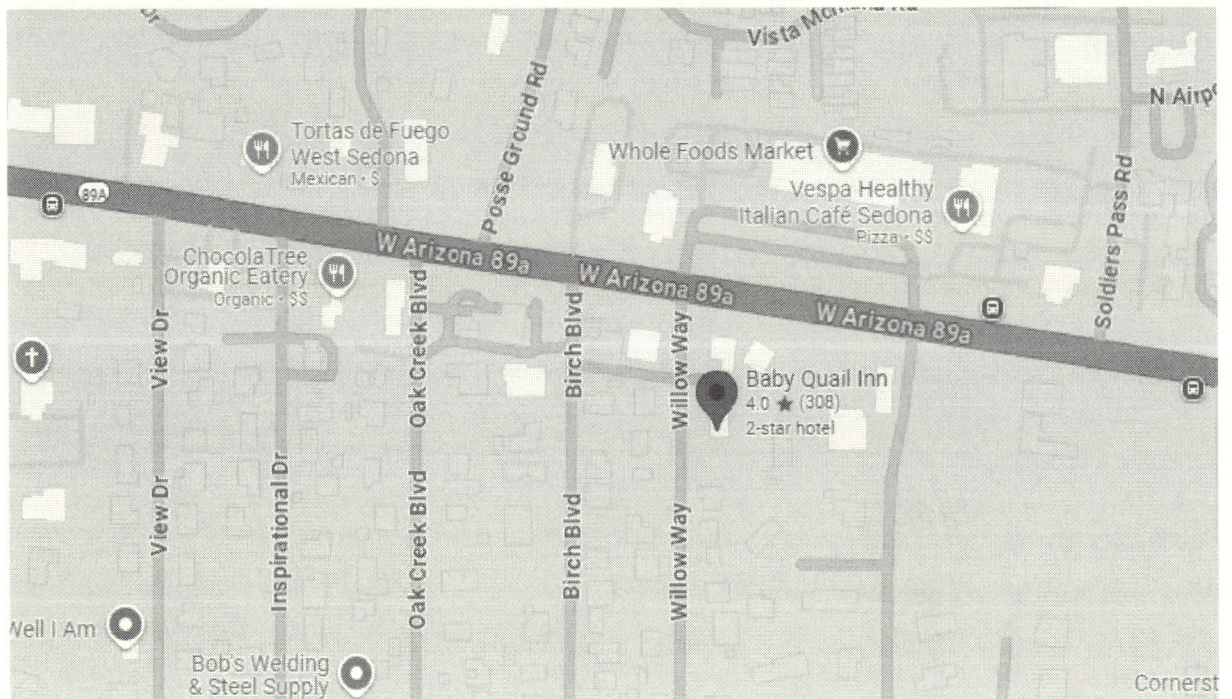

Highlights:
The **Baby Quail Inn** is a quaint, family-run boutique hotel that offers a warm and welcoming atmosphere. Guests can relax in the peaceful garden courtyard or unwind in the hot tub. The inn is located close to Sedona's shops and restaurants, making it a convenient and budget-friendly option for those looking to explore the area.

Pricing:

- Rooms range from $100 to $180 per night, depending on the season.

Location:
50 Willow Way, Sedona, AZ 86336
Map & Directions

Website:
https://www.babyquailinn.com

3. GreenTree Inn Sedona

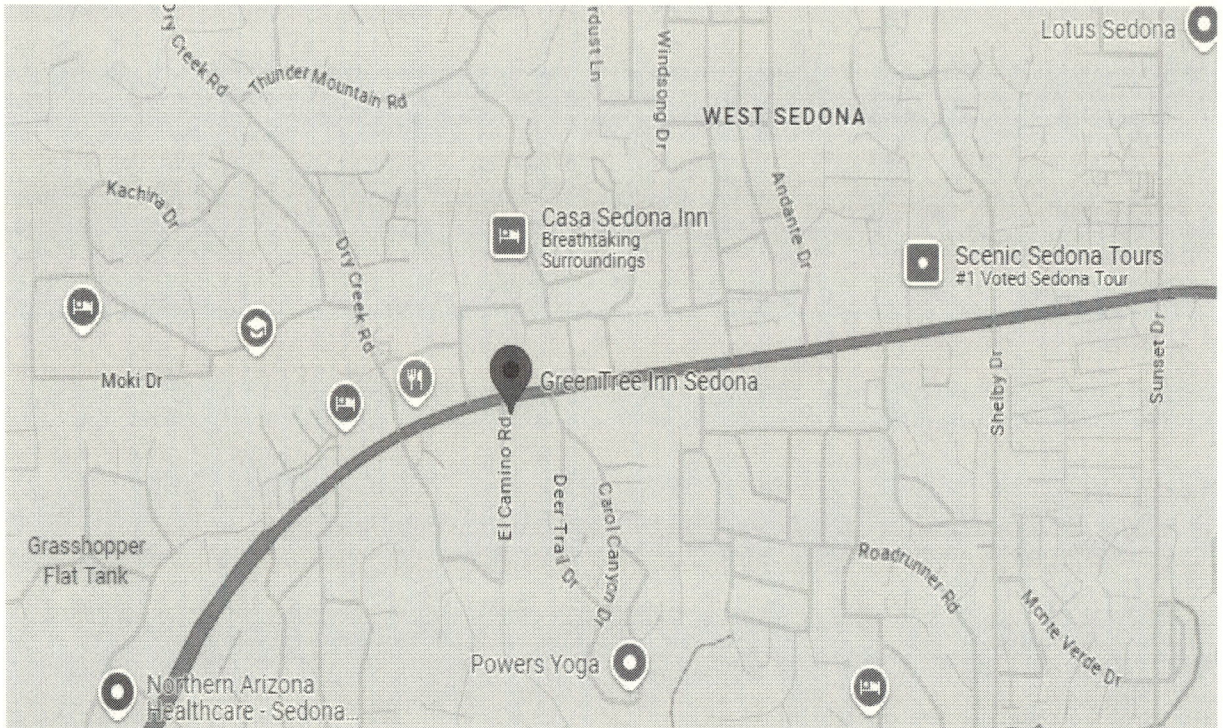

Highlights:

Located near **West Sedona**, the **GreenTree Inn** offers budget accommodations with amenities such as an outdoor pool, hot tub, and complimentary breakfast. Its close proximity to popular trails like **Devil's Bridge** makes it a great choice for nature lovers looking for a cost-effective stay.

Pricing:

- Rooms range from $110 to $220 per night, depending on the season.

Location:

2991 AZ-89A, Sedona, AZ 86336
Map & Directions

Website:

https://www.greentreeinnsedona.com

Best Areas to Stay Based on Activities

Choosing where to stay in Sedona depends on the activities you plan to enjoy during your visit. Different areas offer unique experiences, from hiking and outdoor adventures to shopping and dining.

1. Uptown Sedona (Best for Shopping, Dining, and Sightseeing)

Highlights:
Uptown Sedona is the town's bustling commercial hub, filled with shops, galleries, restaurants, and tour operators. Staying here gives you easy access to Sedona's shopping and dining scene as well as jeep tours and scenic viewpoints.

Recommended Accommodations:

- **Amara Resort and Spa**
- **L'Auberge de Sedona**

2. West Sedona (Best for Hiking and Outdoor Adventures)

Highlights:
West Sedona is ideal for those seeking outdoor activities, with easy access to hiking trails like **Devil's Bridge** and **Soldier Pass**. It's a quieter area with plenty of local restaurants, making it perfect for nature enthusiasts.

Recommended Accommodations:

- **GreenTree Inn Sedona**
- **Sedona Rouge Hotel and Spa**

3. Village of Oak Creek (Best for Scenic Views and Peaceful Getaways)

Highlights:
Just south of Sedona, the **Village of Oak Creek** offers incredible views of landmarks like **Bell Rock** and **Cathedral Rock**. It's a peaceful area with a few excellent restaurants and golf courses, making it ideal for a serene getaway.

Recommended Accommodations:

- **Sedona Village Lodge**
- **Hilton Sedona Resort at Bell Rock**

Sustainable Travel in Sedona

Sedona's striking natural beauty, featuring its iconic red rock formations and peaceful desert landscapes, makes it a popular spot for nature enthusiasts. However, the rising number of visitors has increased the need for sustainable travel practices to protect the environment and maintain the area's unique charm for future generations. By traveling responsibly, you can enjoy Sedona's wonders while minimizing your environmental impact. This section offers eco-friendly travel tips, ways to support local businesses, and suggestions for reducing your environmental footprint during your stay in Sedona.

Eco-Friendly Travel Tips

Sustainable travel begins with making thoughtful decisions that help protect the environment. In Sedona, there are several ways visitors can reduce their environmental impact.

1. Bring Reusable Water Bottles and Containers

Highlights:
Sedona's desert climate makes staying hydrated essential, especially if you're exploring outdoors. Instead of purchasing single-use plastic bottles, bring a reusable water bottle to refill at various refill stations around Sedona. Many hotels and public spaces have refill stations available to help reduce plastic waste.

Additionally, some local shops offer eco-friendly reusable containers made from sustainable materials, which can serve as both a practical item for your trip and a great eco-conscious souvenir.

Pricing:

- Reusable water bottles: $10-$30
- Refill stations: Free at many locations.

Location:
Reusable water bottles are available at local shops, such as:

- **Sedona Refill Station**
  Map & Directions

2. Opt for Sustainable Transportation

Highlights:
Sedona's compact size and proximity to key attractions make it easy to explore on foot, by bike, or via electric vehicle. Choosing walking or cycling over driving helps reduce your carbon footprint, and several rental shops offer both traditional and electric bikes for visitors.

For longer trips, opt for electric vehicles or carpooling services. Many hotels provide electric vehicle (EV) charging stations, making it easier for eco-conscious travelers to get around while minimizing their emissions.

Pricing:

- Bike rentals: $35-$75 per day
- EV charging stations: Free at many hotels for guests.

Location:
Bike rentals can be found at:

- **Sedona Bike & Bean**
  Map & Directions
  https://www.sedonabikeandbean.com

EV charging is available at:

- **Amara Resort and Spa**
  Map & Directions

3. Follow Responsible Hiking and Trail Etiquette

Highlights:
Sedona's extensive network of trails is a major draw, but overuse can negatively impact the delicate desert ecosystem. To minimize your impact, stay on designated paths and avoid wandering off-trail to prevent damaging plants and wildlife habitats. Additionally, always follow **Leave No Trace** principles by packing out any trash, including biodegradable items, and avoid disturbing the natural environment.

You can also consider joining eco-tours led by local operators that promote sustainable practices and provide education on Sedona's unique environment.

Pricing:

- Access to most trails is free, but some require a **Red Rock Pass**: $5 per day, $15 per week, $20 annually.

Location:
Eco-friendly trails include:

- **Cathedral Rock Trail**
  Map & Directions

Eco-tours are offered by:

- **Sedona Eco-Tours**
  https://sedonaecotours.com

Supporting Local Businesses

Supporting local businesses is a vital part of sustainable travel, as it ensures that your spending benefits the local economy. Sedona has a wealth of locally-owned shops, restaurants, and eco-friendly tour companies. By shopping locally and dining at independent establishments, you're helping the community thrive.

1. Buy Sustainable and Local Products

Highlights:
Sedona is home to numerous galleries, boutiques, and shops offering locally made products, including handmade crafts, jewelry, and eco-friendly items. When shopping for souvenirs, choose locally crafted goods or environmentally friendly products made from sustainable materials.

The **Sedona Community Farmers Market** is another excellent spot to support local farmers and artisans. You can find fresh organic produce, locally made foods, and handmade products, all produced with sustainability in mind.

Pricing:

- Farmers Market: Free to enter, with varying prices for goods.
- Local souvenirs: $10-$50, depending on the item.

Location:

- **Sedona Community Farmers Market**
  95 Arroyo Pinon Dr, Sedona, AZ 86336
  Map & Directions

Website:
http://www.sedona-farmers-market.com

2. Dine at Farm-to-Table Restaurants

Highlights:
Sedona boasts a variety of farm-to-table restaurants that prioritize locally sourced ingredients. Eating at these establishments supports local farmers and reduces the carbon footprint associated with food transport. Many of Sedona's restaurants emphasize organic and sustainable produce, offering healthy and eco-conscious meals.

Creekside American Bistro and **Mariposa Latin Inspired Grill** are just a couple of restaurants that highlight seasonal dishes using fresh, local ingredients, providing diners with a farm-fresh experience.

Pricing:

- Farm-to-table meals: $20-$50 per person, depending on the restaurant.

Location:

- **Creekside American Bistro**
  251 AZ-179, Sedona, AZ 86336
  Map & Directions
  https://www.creeksidebistro.com

Minimizing Your Environmental Footprint

To reduce your environmental impact while visiting Sedona, you can focus on conserving energy, reducing waste, and staying at eco-conscious accommodations. By being mindful of how you travel and consume resources, you can help protect Sedona's environment.

1. Stay at Eco-Friendly Accommodations

Highlights:
Several hotels and resorts in Sedona have adopted sustainable practices to lessen their environmental impact. Look for eco-friendly accommodations that prioritize energy efficiency, water conservation, and waste reduction. Some properties have been awarded eco-certifications and offer green initiatives such as solar energy, low-flow water fixtures, and composting.

Resorts like **L'Auberge de Sedona** and **Amara Resort and Spa** prioritize sustainability by offering energy-efficient facilities, water-saving programs, and EV charging stations.

Pricing:

- Eco-friendly accommodations: $400-$1,400 per night, depending on the hotel and season.

Location:

- **L'Auberge de Sedona**
  301 Little Lane, Sedona, AZ 86336
  Map & Directions
  https://www.lauberge.com

2. Conserve Water and Energy

Highlights:
Sedona's desert climate makes water conservation essential. Visitors can conserve water by taking shorter showers, turning off taps while brushing their teeth, and reusing towels and linens at hotels. Many eco-friendly accommodations encourage guests to participate in water-saving efforts.

To conserve energy, turn off lights, air conditioning, and electronics when not in use, and be mindful of your energy consumption throughout your stay.

3. Reduce Waste

Highlights:

Reducing waste is another key element of sustainable travel. Avoid single-use plastics by bringing reusable items, such as water bottles, bags, and utensils. If you're getting food or drinks to-go, opt for recyclable or compostable containers, or bring your own reusable options.

When hiking or visiting outdoor spaces, make sure to pack out all trash and dispose of it responsibly to protect Sedona's ecosystems.

Sedona for Families

Sedona is a fantastic destination for families, offering a mix of outdoor adventures and educational experiences that appeal to visitors of all ages. With scenic landscapes, engaging tours, and hands-on museums, there are plenty of activities to enjoy together as a family. This section highlights the best family-friendly activities, kid-friendly hikes, and educational tours and museums that make Sedona a great place for children and adults alike.

Family-Friendly Activities

Sedona provides an abundance of family-friendly attractions, from exciting outdoor activities to creative and leisurely experiences, ensuring that everyone in the family has something to enjoy.

1. Slide Rock State Park

Highlights:
A top family destination in Sedona, **Slide Rock State Park** offers a natural water park where kids and adults alike can slide down the smooth rock formations in Oak Creek. It's the perfect place for families to cool off, swim, and enjoy a picnic surrounded by Sedona's stunning red rocks. The park is also ideal for short hikes and exploration.

With natural rock slides, wading areas, and plenty of picnic spots, families can easily spend a fun-filled day at this unique location.

Pricing:

- $10 per vehicle on weekdays, $20 per vehicle on weekends and holidays.

Location:
6871 AZ-89A, Sedona, AZ 86336
Map & Directions

2. Pink Jeep Tours

Highlights:
Pink Jeep Tours provide families with an exciting off-road adventure through Sedona's red rock landscapes. With knowledgeable guides leading the way, these tours are not only thrilling but educational as well, with information about Sedona's geology, history, and wildlife. Popular options like the **Broken Arrow** and **Ancient Ruins** tours allow families to explore Sedona's stunning scenery and learn about the area's rich past.

The guided tours offer an exciting experience for kids, with plenty of chances to ask questions and learn interesting facts about the region.

Pricing:

- Tours range from $125 to $150 per person, with family packages available.

Location:
204 N State Route 89A, Sedona, AZ 86336
Map & Directions

3. Sedona Trolley

Highlights:
For families looking for a more relaxed way to see the sights, the **Sedona Trolley** offers a comfortable tour through Sedona's scenic landscapes and cultural districts. The open-air trolley provides a fun way to explore while learning about Sedona's history and geology through guided narration, making it an engaging experience for kids.

Families can choose between two different tour routes, each highlighting Sedona's famous landmarks and scenic vistas.

Pricing:

- $29 per adult, $18 per child (ages 5-12), free for children under 5.

Location:
276 N State Route 89A, Sedona, AZ 86336
Map & Directions

Website:
https://sedonatrolley.com

Kid-Friendly Hikes and Outdoor Adventures

Sedona offers a variety of easy, scenic hiking trails that are perfect for families with children. These kid-friendly hikes are manageable and offer great opportunities for outdoor exploration in Sedona's beautiful red rock environment.

1. Bell Rock Pathway

Highlights:
Bell Rock Pathway is an excellent choice for families, featuring a wide, relatively flat trail that offers spectacular views of **Bell Rock** and **Courthouse Butte**. This 3.6-mile trail is easy enough for younger kids and allows families to hike as much or as little as they prefer, making it a flexible and fun option for all ages.

Children will love climbing rocks and crossing small streams along the way, and the trail offers ample opportunities for photo stops.

Pricing:

- A **Red Rock Pass** is required for parking: $5 per day, $15 per week, $20 annually.

Location:
Bell Rock Trailhead, Village of Oak Creek, Sedona, AZ 86351
Map & Directions

2. West Fork Trail

Highlights:
For a more shaded, creek-side adventure, **West Fork Trail** in Oak Creek Canyon is a fantastic option. This 6.5-mile round-trip hike is known for its cooler temperatures,

lush greenery, and multiple creek crossings, providing plenty of exploration opportunities for children. Families can enjoy a leisurely hike through the canyon, with stunning views of towering cliffs and plenty of places to dip toes in the creek.

West Fork is a family favorite, particularly during warmer months, and offers a great escape into nature with its easy-to-follow path.

Pricing:

- Parking fee: $11 per vehicle.

Location:
Oak Creek Canyon, Sedona, AZ 86336
Map & Directions

3. Fay Canyon Trail

Highlights:
Fay Canyon Trail is a gentle, 2.4-mile round-trip hike through a beautiful red rock canyon, making it an ideal trail for families with younger kids. The flat, easy-to-navigate path is surrounded by towering canyon walls, and the hike's endpoint offers great views and a chance for kids to climb rocks and explore.

The shaded trail and simple terrain make this a perfect introductory hike for children, allowing them to enjoy the beauty of Sedona's red rocks without much effort.

Pricing:

- A **Red Rock Pass** is required for parking: $5 per day, $15 per week, $20 annually.

Location:
Boynton Pass Rd, Sedona, AZ 86336
Map & Directions

Educational Tours and Museums

Sedona also offers several educational attractions that families can enjoy together, where children can learn about the region's history, culture, and natural environment.

1. Sedona Heritage Museum

Highlights:
The **Sedona Heritage Museum** provides families with an engaging look at Sedona's history, including exhibits on early settlers, Native American culture, and the town's ties to Hollywood. With interactive displays and special programs, the museum offers a hands-on experience that's both fun and educational for children.

The museum also hosts seasonal events and reenactments, providing families with additional opportunities to learn about Sedona's rich past.

Pricing:

- $7 for adults, $3 for children (ages 6-17), free for children under 6.

Location:
735 Jordan Rd, Sedona, AZ 86336
Map & Directions

Website:
https://sedonamuseum.org

2. Palatki Heritage Site

Highlights:
At the **Palatki Heritage Site**, families can explore ancient Sinagua cliff dwellings and rock art, gaining insight into the lives of the people who inhabited the area over 800 years ago. The site offers guided tours where kids can learn about archaeology and history, all while seeing ancient pictographs up close.

It's a fascinating and educational experience for families, allowing children to connect with the region's cultural heritage.

Pricing:

- $5 per person, free for children under 16.

Location:
Forest Rd 525, Sedona, AZ 86336
Map & Directions

3. Lowell Observatory

Highlights:
Located in nearby Flagstaff, **Lowell Observatory** offers a fantastic opportunity for families interested in space and astronomy. Known for its role in the discovery of Pluto, the observatory features interactive exhibits, educational programs for kids, and opportunities to observe the night sky through powerful telescopes.

With guided tours and stargazing sessions, it's an exciting way for children to learn about space and science in a fun, hands-on setting.

Pricing:

- $25 for adults, $15 for children (ages 5-17), free for children under 5.

Location:
1400 W Mars Hill Rd, Flagstaff, AZ 86001
Map & Directions

Website:
https://lowell.edu

Sedona for Couples

Sedona is a perfect romantic escape, offering stunning natural beauty, serene landscapes, and a range of intimate experiences for couples. Whether celebrating a honeymoon, anniversary, or simply looking for a peaceful retreat, Sedona's romantic spots, breathtaking sunset views, and luxurious spa experiences make it an ideal destination. This section explores top romantic locations, the best places to enjoy sunsets, and rejuvenating spa and wellness options tailored for couples seeking memorable moments together.

Romantic Spots and Activities

Sedona's captivating scenery provides the perfect setting for couples to enjoy romantic activities, from scenic hikes to peaceful picnics and quiet time surrounded by majestic red rock formations.

1. Cathedral Rock Vortex

Highlights:
Cathedral Rock is one of Sedona's most famous landmarks and a popular romantic spot. Couples can hike the **Cathedral Rock Trail**, which offers moderate difficulty and leads to a spectacular viewpoint ideal for taking in the stunning surroundings. The serene energy of the **Cathedral Rock Vortex** makes it an excellent spot for couples looking to reconnect while enjoying the breathtaking views.

This location is particularly magical at sunset, as the golden glow of the setting sun illuminates the red rocks, creating a truly romantic atmosphere.

Pricing:

- A **Red Rock Pass** is required for parking: $5 per day, $15 per week, $20 annually.

Location:
Cathedral Rock Trailhead, Back O' Beyond Rd, Sedona, AZ 86336
Map & Directions

2. Crescent Moon Picnic Area and Red Rock Crossing

Highlights:
Couples seeking a relaxed and romantic setting should visit **Crescent Moon Picnic Area** at **Red Rock Crossing**, where the flowing waters of Oak Creek reflect the majestic Cathedral Rock. This scenic spot is perfect for an intimate picnic with a view of one of Sedona's most iconic landmarks. Couples can also enjoy a peaceful walk along the creek, take photos, and dip their toes in the water while soaking in the picturesque scenery.

As one of the most photographed places in Sedona, Red Rock Crossing provides an idyllic backdrop for couples looking to capture their special moments together.

Pricing:

- Day-use fee: $11 per vehicle.

Location:
300 Red Rock Crossing Rd, Sedona, AZ 86336
Map & Directions

3. Tlaquepaque Arts & Shopping Village

Highlights:
For a charming, romantic day out, couples can explore **Tlaquepaque Arts & Shopping Village**. Modeled after a traditional Mexican village, this picturesque spot is filled with art galleries, boutique shops, and lush courtyards. Couples can stroll along cobblestone paths, admire the local artwork, or enjoy a meal in one of the village's inviting cafes.

With its ivy-covered archways and flower-filled courtyards, Tlaquepaque offers a peaceful and romantic atmosphere for couples looking to explore art and culture together.

Pricing:

- Entry to Tlaquepaque is free; prices vary at shops and restaurants.

Location:
336 AZ-179, Sedona, AZ 86336
Map & Directions

Website:
https://www.tlaq.com

Best Sunset Views

Sedona is famous for its stunning sunsets, where the red rocks come to life in vibrant colors. Couples can enjoy this magical time from several romantic locations, each offering unforgettable views of the sun setting behind the rugged landscape.

1. Airport Mesa

Highlights:
Airport Mesa is one of the best places in Sedona to watch the sunset. With panoramic views of the red rocks, including **Cathedral Rock**, **Bell Rock**, and **Courthouse Butte**, it's a popular spot for couples to witness the breathtaking glow of the sun as it dips behind the horizon. Whether you drive up to the **Airport Mesa Overlook** or hike the **Airport Loop Trail**, this location provides an unforgettable sunset experience.

Pricing:

- Parking fee: $3 at the Airport Mesa parking lot.

Location:
483 Airport Rd, Sedona, AZ 86336
Map & Directions

2. Doe Mountain Trail

Highlights:

For a more secluded sunset experience, the **Doe Mountain Trail** offers couples a peaceful alternative. This 1.5-mile hike leads to a flat mesa, where you'll enjoy sweeping views of the surrounding red rock formations. At the summit, couples can share a private moment as they watch the sky light up in shades of pink and orange, making it a perfect setting for a quiet and romantic evening.

Pricing:

- A **Red Rock Pass** is required for parking: $5 per day, $15 per week, $20 annually.

Location:

Doe Mountain Trailhead, Boynton Pass Rd, Sedona, AZ 86336
Map & Directions

3. Sedona Vortex Sites

Highlights:

Sedona's famous vortex sites, such as **Bell Rock** and **Boynton Canyon**, not only offer spiritual energy but also incredible sunset views. These peaceful spots allow couples to enjoy the sunset while feeling connected to Sedona's unique atmosphere. The serene setting at these vortex sites makes them ideal for couples who want to experience both natural beauty and the calming energy that Sedona is known for.

Pricing:

- A **Red Rock Pass** is required for parking at most vortex locations: $5 per day, $15 per week, $20 annually.

Location:

Vortex sites like Bell Rock, Boynton Canyon, and Cathedral Rock are easily accessible from Sedona's trailheads.

Spa and Wellness Experiences for Couples

Sedona's wellness culture is perfect for couples looking to relax and rejuvenate. From world-class spa treatments to tranquil meditation experiences, Sedona offers a wide range of options for couples to unwind and reconnect.

1. Mii amo Spa at Enchantment Resort

Highlights:
Mii amo Spa at **Enchantment Resort** is a top destination for couples seeking a luxurious spa experience. Nestled in **Boynton Canyon**, this world-class spa offers a range of treatments designed for couples, including massages, body treatments, and holistic wellness experiences inspired by Native American traditions. For a more immersive experience, couples can book a multi-day retreat that focuses on relaxation, healing, and reconnecting.

Mii amo's peaceful setting and transformative treatments make it a perfect place for couples to indulge in a deeply rejuvenating experience.

Pricing:

- Treatments range from $150 to $500 per person. Multi-day retreat pricing varies by package.

Location:
525 Boynton Canyon Rd, Sedona, AZ 86336
Map & Directions

Website:
https://www.miiamo.com

2. L'Auberge de Sedona Spa

Highlights:
Set along the serene banks of **Oak Creek**, the spa at **L'Auberge de Sedona** offers couples the chance to unwind in a peaceful natural setting. Specializing in personalized treatments, the spa provides couples' massages, body treatments, and facials, with the option of enjoying a **Creekside Massage** in a private cabana by the

water. This unique experience, surrounded by nature, enhances relaxation and allows couples to connect in a peaceful environment.

Pricing:

- Couples' massages start at $350.

Location:
301 Little Lane, Sedona, AZ 86336
Map & Directions

3. Amara Resort and Spa

Highlights:
For a modern and stylish spa experience, **Amara Resort and Spa** offers couples a variety of treatments, including massages, facials, and body wraps. The spa uses locally sourced ingredients, creating a unique Sedona-inspired experience. Couples can also relax in the infinity pool or hot tub, enjoying views of **Snoopy Rock** as they unwind together.

Amara's blend of luxury and tranquility makes it a great choice for couples looking to refresh and rejuvenate during their Sedona stay.

Pricing:

- Couples' massages start at $300.

Location:
100 Amara Ln, Sedona, AZ 86336
Map & Directions

Website:
https://www.amararesort.com

Practical Tips for Visiting Sedona

Sedona is a stunning destination known for its red rock formations, hiking trails, and spiritual energy. Whether you're visiting for outdoor activities, relaxation, or a mix of both, being well-prepared can help you make the most of your trip. This guide provides practical tips on what to pack, staying safe during outdoor adventures, and dealing with Sedona's high altitudes.

Packing Essentials for Sedona

To enjoy Sedona's unique desert environment, it's important to pack wisely for the varying weather conditions and outdoor adventures you may encounter. Here's a rundown of what you'll need.

1. Layered Clothing

Highlights:
Sedona's temperatures can fluctuate significantly throughout the day. Days are often warm, while mornings and evenings can be cool, especially in spring and fall. Pack light, moisture-wicking clothing that you can layer, along with a jacket or fleece for cooler times of the day.

In the summer, light, breathable fabrics are essential, along with a wide-brimmed hat and sunglasses for sun protection. In winter, bring warmer layers to stay comfortable during chilly nights.

Pricing:

- Lightweight shirts and pants: $30-$60
- Jackets or fleeces: $40-$100

2. Sun Protection

Highlights:
Sedona's high desert elevation means stronger sun exposure, so sun protection is a must. Bring sunscreen with high SPF, a wide-brimmed hat, and UV-protective sunglasses. Consider wearing long sleeves during hikes to shield yourself from the sun.

Even on cooler days, the sun can be intense, so be sure to reapply sunscreen regularly.

Pricing:

- Sunscreen (SPF 30+): $10-$20
- Wide-brimmed hats: $20-$40

3. Reusable Water Bottle and Hydration Gear

Highlights:
Hydration is key in Sedona's dry climate, especially if you're hiking. Be sure to bring a reusable water bottle or hydration pack. Many trails lack water refill stations, so carrying enough water is crucial, particularly for long hikes.

It's recommended to bring 1-2 liters of water per person for a typical day hike, with more for longer or more strenuous hikes.

Pricing:

- Reusable water bottles: $10-$30
- Hydration packs: $40-$100

4. Sturdy Hiking Shoes

Highlights:
Given Sedona's rugged and uneven terrain, a sturdy pair of hiking shoes or boots with good grip and ankle support is essential. The trails can be rocky, so comfortable, durable footwear is key to enjoying your outdoor adventures. Trail runners may also be an option for shorter, easier hikes.

Make sure to break in new shoes before your trip to avoid discomfort or blisters.

Pricing:

- Hiking shoes or boots: $60-$150

5. Maps and Navigation Tools

Highlights:
Although many of Sedona's trails are well-marked, it's a good idea to bring a physical map or download trail maps to your phone for offline use. Cell service can be spotty in some areas, so having a backup map or GPS is recommended.

You can pick up maps at visitor centers or use apps like **AllTrails** or **Gaia GPS** to navigate the trails.

Pricing:

- Paper maps: $5-$10
- Trail map apps: Free to $30/year for premium features.

Safety Tips for Hiking and Outdoor Activities

While Sedona offers incredible opportunities for outdoor activities, it's important to stay safe, especially when hiking or exploring the desert's more remote areas.

1. Stick to Designated Trails

Highlights:
To protect both the environment and yourself, it's important to stay on marked trails. Going off-trail can damage the ecosystem and increase the risk of getting lost or encountering dangerous terrain. Many trails, like **Cathedral Rock**, **Bell Rock Pathway**, and **Devil's Bridge**, are well-marked and popular, but always check maps at trailheads to ensure you're following the right route.

Pricing:

- Free access to most trails, though some require a **Red Rock Pass**: $5 per day, $15 per week, $20 annually.

2. Carry Plenty of Water

Highlights:
With Sedona's dry climate and high elevation, it's easy to become dehydrated. Always carry more water than you think you'll need, as most trails don't have water

refill stations. For longer hikes, 1-2 liters per person is recommended, and electrolyte drinks or tablets can help replenish lost minerals.

Avoid alcohol and caffeinated drinks before hikes, as they can increase dehydration.

Pricing:

- Electrolyte drinks or tablets: $10-$20

3. Be Aware of Wildlife

Highlights:
Although encounters are rare, Sedona is home to wildlife like snakes, coyotes, and bobcats. If you spot wildlife on the trail, keep a respectful distance and avoid feeding or approaching the animals. Rattlesnakes are common in warmer months, so stay alert, especially when stepping over rocks or through tall grass.

Pricing:

- Safety gear like whistles or first aid kits: $10-$25

4. Monitor Weather Conditions

Highlights:
Desert weather can be unpredictable. Check the forecast before heading out and be prepared for sudden changes in temperature. In the summer, aim to start hikes early in the morning to avoid the intense midday heat. In winter, be cautious of snow or ice at higher elevations, especially on shaded trails.

Monsoon season, which runs from July to September, can bring sudden thunderstorms and flash floods. Avoid low-lying areas and seek shelter if storm clouds appear.

Pricing:

- Weather-appropriate gear (rain jackets, hats, etc.): $30-$70

Navigating High Altitudes

Sedona sits at an elevation of 4,300 to 5,000 feet, which can affect visitors not used to higher altitudes. To avoid altitude sickness, it's important to take a few precautions.

1. Gradual Acclimation

Highlights:
If you're coming from lower elevations, give yourself time to adjust to Sedona's altitude. Take it easy on your first day and avoid intense physical activities until you've had time to acclimate. Drink extra water to stay hydrated, as higher altitudes can increase dehydration.

2. Recognizing Altitude Sickness

Highlights:
Altitude sickness can occur at higher elevations and symptoms include headaches, dizziness, nausea, and shortness of breath. If you experience any of these symptoms, rest, hydrate, and avoid further physical exertion. Most mild cases will improve as your body adjusts, but descending to lower elevations may be necessary if symptoms persist.

3. Take Breaks During Outdoor Activities

Highlights:
Hiking at higher altitudes can feel more strenuous due to the reduced oxygen levels. Take frequent breaks and don't rush. For longer hikes like **West Fork Trail** or **Bear Mountain**, start slowly and rest often to allow your body to adjust.

Pricing:

- Most trails are free to access, though some require a **Red Rock Pass**: $5 per day, $15 per week, $20 annually.

Itineraries for Every Traveler

Sedona's stunning red rock landscapes and vibrant culture make it an exciting destination for any traveler, whether you're here for a quick visit or an extended stay. Whether you're into hiking, exploring art galleries, or relaxing with some wellness treatments, Sedona has something for everyone. In this guide, we'll explore various itineraries to help you make the most of your time, whether you're visiting for 1 day, 3 days, or 5 days. Each itinerary includes a mix of outdoor activities, cultural experiences, and relaxation.

1-Day Sedona Itinerary: A Snapshot of Sedona

If you're limited to one day in Sedona, you'll want to focus on experiencing some of the most iconic highlights, from red rock views to a taste of local art and culture. This itinerary is ideal for those passing through or looking for a quick Sedona adventure.

Morning: Hike Cathedral Rock

Begin your day with a visit to one of Sedona's most iconic landmarks: **Cathedral Rock**. The **Cathedral Rock Trail** is a short but moderately steep hike that rewards you with incredible views of Sedona's red rock formations. This location is also a well-known energy vortex site, providing an opportunity to feel the area's spiritual energy while enjoying the breathtaking surroundings.

Pricing:

- A **Red Rock Pass** is required for parking: $5 per day.

Location:
Cathedral Rock Trailhead, Back O' Beyond Rd, Sedona, AZ 86336
Map & Directions

Lunch: Creekside American Bistro

After your hike, enjoy a meal at **Creekside American Bistro**, which offers beautiful views of Oak Creek and Sedona's red rocks. The restaurant features a menu with locally sourced ingredients, making it a perfect place to relax and recharge while savoring delicious food.

Pricing:

- Main dishes: $15-$25

Location:
251 AZ-179, Sedona, AZ 86336
Map & Directions

Website:
https://www.creeksidebistro.com

Afternoon: Tlaquepaque Arts & Shopping Village

Spend the afternoon exploring the charming **Tlaquepaque Arts & Shopping Village**, which offers a collection of galleries, artisan shops, and restaurants. Stroll through its cobblestone paths and enjoy the serene atmosphere, where you can admire local art, handmade crafts, and jewelry.

Pricing:

- Entrance is free; prices vary for shopping and dining.

Location:
336 AZ-179, Sedona, AZ 86336
Map & Directions

Website:
https://www.tlaq.com

Sunset: Airport Mesa Overlook

Conclude your day by watching the sunset at **Airport Mesa Overlook**, one of the best places to enjoy the sun setting over Sedona's iconic red rocks. The overlook offers panoramic views of famous rock formations, including **Cathedral Rock** and **Bell Rock**, creating a magical scene as the landscape glows with the setting sun.

Pricing:

- Parking fee: $3 at the Airport Mesa lot.

Location:
483 Airport Rd, Sedona, AZ 86336
Map & Directions

3-Day Sedona Itinerary: A More In-Depth Experience

With three days in Sedona, you'll have the chance to explore a wider range of activities, including more hikes, spiritual vortex visits, and some time to relax at one of Sedona's famous wellness centers.

Day 1: Hiking and Scenic Views

Morning: Hike Devil's Bridge
Start your first day with a hike to **Devil's Bridge**, the largest natural sandstone arch in Sedona. This moderately challenging hike covers 4.2 miles round-trip, but the view from the top is absolutely worth it. You'll have the opportunity to take photos on the arch with breathtaking views of the red rocks all around.

Pricing:

- A **Red Rock Pass** is required for parking: $5 per day.

Location:
Devil's Bridge Trailhead, Dry Creek Rd, Sedona, AZ 86336
Map & Directions

Afternoon: Lunch at Mariposa Latin Inspired Grill
After your hike, enjoy lunch at **Mariposa Latin Inspired Grill**, where you can dine with stunning views of Sedona's red rocks. The restaurant serves a Latin American-inspired menu made with fresh, local ingredients.

Pricing:

- Main dishes: $20-$40

Location:
700 AZ-89A, Sedona, AZ 86336
Map & Directions

Website:
https://mariposasedona.com

Evening: Stargazing at Evening Sky Tours
Sedona's clear night skies make it a prime location for stargazing. Book a tour with **Evening Sky Tours**, where professional astronomers will guide you through the constellations and celestial bodies using high-powered telescopes.

Pricing:

- Tours cost $100 per person.

Location:
Sedona, AZ
Map & Directions

Website:
https://www.eveningskytours.com

Day 2: Exploring Sedona's Spiritual Side

Morning: Visit Bell Rock and Courthouse Butte Vortex
On day two, explore the energy vortexes at **Bell Rock** and **Courthouse Butte**. You can hike the 4-mile **Bell Rock Pathway** or take a more leisurely walk around the base, enjoying the views while absorbing the calming energy of these famous formations.

Pricing:

- A **Red Rock Pass** is required for parking: $5 per day.

Location:
Bell Rock Trailhead, Village of Oak Creek, Sedona, AZ 86351
Map & Directions

Afternoon: Lunch and Spa Day at L'Auberge de Sedona
Head to **L'Auberge de Sedona** for a peaceful lunch at **Cress on Oak Creek**. Afterward, indulge in a relaxing spa treatment with a couples' massage or other rejuvenating services, all in the beautiful creekside setting of this luxury resort.

Pricing:

- Main dishes: $20-$35
- Spa treatments: $150-$400

Location:
301 Little Lane, Sedona, AZ 86336
Map & Directions

Website:
https://www.lauberge.com

Day 3: Arts and Culture Exploration

Morning: Visit Sedona Arts Center

Spend the morning exploring the **Sedona Arts Center**, where you can browse art exhibits and workshops from local artists. The gallery offers a variety of paintings, pottery, and jewelry, perfect for discovering Sedona's creative culture.

Pricing:

- Entry is free, but prices vary for art purchases.

Location:

15 Art Barn Rd, Sedona, AZ 86336
Map & Directions

Website:

https://sedonaartscenter.org

Afternoon: Scenic Drive Through Oak Creek Canyon

After lunch, take a scenic drive through **Oak Creek Canyon**, one of Arizona's most beautiful routes. You'll pass through towering cliffs and lush forests, making stops to enjoy the incredible views.

Pricing:

- Free to drive through Oak Creek Canyon.

5-Day Sedona Itinerary: A Complete Sedona Experience

With five days in Sedona, you'll have ample time to experience the best of Sedona, from top hikes to relaxing spa days and everything in between.

Day 1: Relaxation and Dinner

Settle in and enjoy a relaxing evening with dinner at **Elote Café**, which offers upscale Mexican cuisine with scenic views of Sedona's red rocks.

Pricing:

- Main dishes: $15-$35

Location:
350 Jordan Rd, Sedona, AZ 86336
Map & Directions

Website:
https://www.elotecafe.com

Day 2: Outdoor Exploration

Hike the beautiful **West Fork Trail** in **Oak Creek Canyon**. This 6.5-mile trail follows Oak Creek and offers scenic views of forests, cliffs, and the creek, providing a more shaded hike compared to other trails in the area.

Pricing:

- Parking fee: $11 per vehicle.

Location:
Oak Creek Canyon, Sedona, AZ 86336
Map & Directions

Day 3: Spiritual Wellness

Visit **Boynton Canyon** to experience one of Sedona's most powerful vortexes. Afterward, head to **Mii amo Spa** at **Enchantment Resort** for a day of wellness treatments, including massages and holistic therapies inspired by Native American healing traditions.

Pricing:

- Spa treatments: $150-$500

Location:
525 Boynton Canyon Rd, Sedona, AZ 86336
Map & Directions

Website:
https://www.miiamo.com

Day 4: Art and Shopping

Spend the day exploring Sedona's art galleries and shopping at **Tlaquepaque Arts & Shopping Village**. Take your time browsing the work of local artists and enjoy lunch at one of the village's charming restaurants.

Day 5: Hot Air Balloon Ride and Farewell

Cap off your Sedona experience with a **hot air balloon ride**, offering a bird's-eye view of Sedona's breathtaking landscapes. Afterward, enjoy a leisurely brunch before departing.

Pricing:

- Hot air balloon rides: $250-$300 per person.

Website:

https://www.redrockballoons.com

Final Thoughts: Make the Most of Your Sedona Adventure

Sedona is a truly magical destination, blending breathtaking natural beauty, outdoor adventure, and a rich cultural scene. Whether you're hiking the iconic red rocks, indulging in a luxurious spa treatment, or soaking in the spiritual energy of its famed vortexes, Sedona offers a unique and unforgettable experience for every traveler. To make the most of your adventure, be sure to embrace a balance of activity and relaxation, take in the stunning sunsets, and immerse yourself in the creative and spiritual vibe that makes Sedona so special.

No matter how long your visit, Sedona's variety of outdoor activities, arts, dining, and wellness experiences will ensure that you leave feeling inspired and rejuvenated. Be mindful of the weather, pack accordingly, stay hydrated, and follow local guidelines to ensure both safety and enjoyment during your trip. Whether it's a day, a weekend, or a full week, Sedona promises to captivate your heart and create lasting memories that will call you back to its red rock paradise time and again.

Safe travels and enjoy every moment of your Sedona journey!

Made in the USA
Las Vegas, NV
03 February 2025